Quiltings, Frolicks & Bees

100 YEARS OF SIGNATURE QUILTS

Sue Reich

Schiffer Publishing Ltd

4880 Lower Valley Road • Atglen, PA 19310

Other Schiffer Books By The Author:
World War II Quilts
ISBN:978-0-7643-3451-1 $39.99
Quilting News of Yesteryear: Crazy as a Bed Quilt
ISBN:978-0-7643-2795-7 $25.95
Quilting News of Yesteryear: 1,000 Pieces and Counting
ISBN:978-0-7643-2595-7 $25.95

Copyright © 2012 by Sue Reich

Library of Congress Control Number: 2012937360

All rights reserved. No part of this work may be reproduced or used in any form or by any means—graphic, electronic, or mechanical, including photocopying or information storage and retrieval systems—without written permission from the publisher.

The scanning, uploading and distribution of this book or any part thereof via the Internet or via any other means without the permission of the publisher is illegal and punishable by law. Please purchase only authorized editions and do not participate in or encourage the electronic piracy of copyrighted materials.

"Schiffer," "Schiffer Publishing Ltd. & Design," and the "Design of pen and inkwell" are registered trademarks of Schiffer Publishing Ltd.

Cover by Bruce Waters
Type set in Ruritania/Minion Pro

ISBN: 978-0-7643-4098-7
Printed in China

Schiffer Books are available at special discounts for bulk purchases for sales promotions or premiums. Special editions, including personalized covers, corporate imprints, and excerpts can be created in large quantities for special needs. For more information contact the publisher:

Published by Schiffer Publishing Ltd.
4880 Lower Valley Road
Atglen, PA 19310
Phone: (610) 593-1777; Fax: (610) 593-2002
E-mail: Info@schifferbooks.com

For the largest selection of fine reference books on this and related subjects, please visit our website at **www.schifferbooks.com**
We are always looking for people to write books on new and related subjects. If you have an idea for a book, please contact us at proposals@schifferbooks.com

This book may be purchased from the publisher.
Please try your bookstore first.
You may write for a free catalog.

In Europe, Schiffer books are distributed by
Bushwood Books
6 Marksbury Ave.
Kew Gardens
Surrey TW9 4JF England
Phone: 44 (0) 20 8392 8585; Fax: 44 (0) 20 8392 9876
E-mail: info@bushwoodbooks.co.uk
Website: www.bushwoodbooks.co.uk

This book is dedicated
to the quiltmakers of yesteryear who
signed and dated their quilts.

Contents

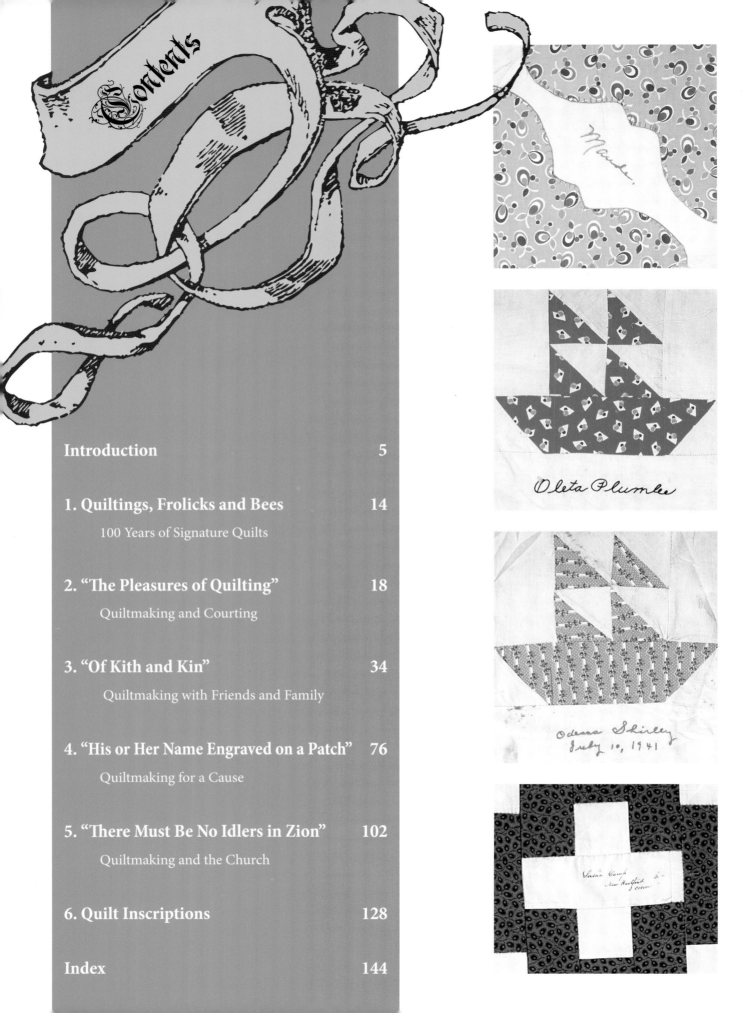

Introduction

The Quilting Bee as represented at *Infinite Variety: Three Centuries of Red and White Quilts*, March 25–30, 2011, New York City, New York.

Quilting is an age-old practice of women gathering together to make bed coverings. They came together in groups for female companionship, fellowship and the need to be together. Often, they assembled to increase their work force and for expediency to get a quilt done. Their quilting communities encompassed families, church groups, civic and social organizations. Through their quiltmaking skills, women comforted both their families and those in need. They successfully raised monies for their villages and towns, for veterans and orphaned children, for worldwide organizations such as the Red Cross, and for benevolent causes close to home. Throughout the nineteenth and twentieth centuries, they applied their needle-arts skills to raise social awareness and end slavery in our country, to advance the sobriety of their spouses and community through the Temperance movement, to lead the charge for womens' right to vote, and to bring awareness to the tragedy and heartbreak of the Aids epidemic.

Inscribed with paint on the back of a Crazy Quilt.

The Meetinghouse Quilters, Washington, Connecticut, 1995.

Historically, the particular names women chose to identify their quilting groups frequently reflected their purpose. Records of the Ladies Benevolent Society of Northfield, Connecticut, span forty-four years—from the second quarter to the fourth quarter of the nineteenth century. Their weekly activities included quilting and the production of clothing and bed linens. Initially, they packed boxes for the Home Missions of the Congregational Church. During the Civil War, supplying provisions for soldiers from the Litchfield Hills and filling quotas of the Sanitary Commission became their main focus. The group's post-Civil War activities benefited veterans and the "Home for the Friendless." By 1879, their quiltmaking raised funds for a new kitchen in the basement of the church and the group's name was changed to "The Ladies Improvement Society." Their weekly reports ended in 1886 when the now-named "Old Sewing Society" still worked on quilts. They also tacked and bound or tied comforters when they met.

More descriptive and creative titles for guilds did not begin until the turn of the twentieth century. One very popular name, especially in German communities, was "Swastika Quilt Guild," but the swastika's use during World War II caused the disappearance of this specific designation. The name "swastika" and symbol, meaning "Good Luck," can be found in ancient civilizations in Asia and the American Indian culture. Today, however, it is forever banned in Germany.

The names selected by groups of women gathered together for the purpose of quilting have always fascinated me. In Washington, Connecticut, my own local group is known as The Meetinghouse Quilters, the name being chosen because our first meetings occurred at the First Congregational Church, and Congregational Churches across New England are referred to as Meetinghouses.

Many quilt guilds select their names from their geographic locales. In New England, with its mountains and rivers, you find a number of guilds with "valley" in their names, such as Heart of the Valley Quilt Guild in Connecticut, Hands Across the Valley Quilters Guild and the Merrimack Valley Quilters Guild in Massachusetts. The Thimble Pleasures Quilting Guild of Massachusetts and Maine's Come Spring Quilters evoke feelings and emotions of quiltmakers and their environment. One of the most intriguing of New England guild names is The Darien Good Wives. This group selected their name, not because they are obedient spouses, but for the Good Wife River that runs through the town of Darien into Long Island Sound.

Uniquely expressive quilt guild names are not restricted to New England. Across the nation, you can find such guilds as:

The Batting Brigade Quilters Guild, Florence, AL
Quilters Above the Clouds, Woodland Park, CO
Material Girls Quilt Club, Coffeyville, KS
Knot Sew Perfect Quilt Guild, Hobart, OK
Prickly Piecers We, Phoenix, AZ
Delmarvalous Quilters Guild, Georgetown, DE
The Needle and Gun Club, Moorestown, NJ

Postcard from the early twentieth century.

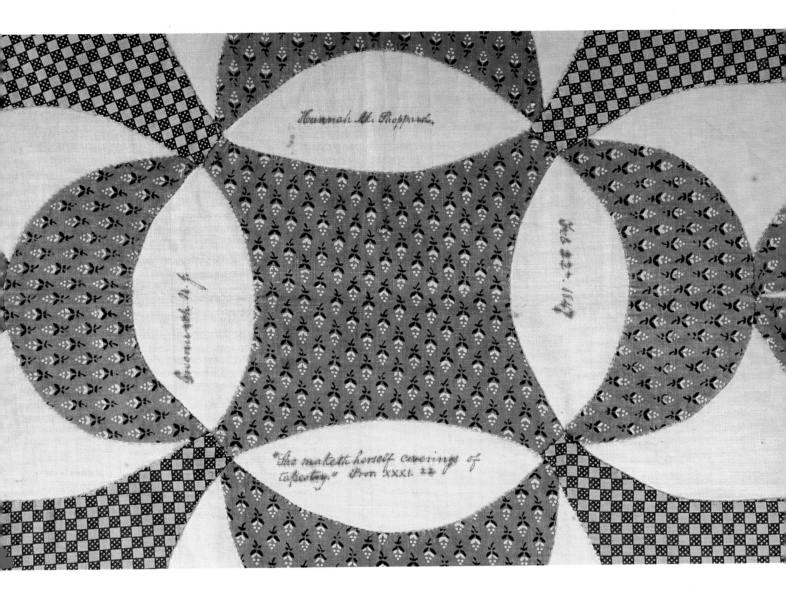

These playful, whimsical identifiers reflect the personalities and purposes of the particular guilds.

My study of historical newspaper articles about women gathering together to quilt and my deep love of signature quilts were the inspirations for writing this book. This genre of quilts has been popular history since the late 1830s. Through the use of pattern, fabric, and the placement of inscribed names, signature quilts give us glimpses of the sociological climates of the times. Often, with just a few clues yielded from these textile documents created with stitches and scroll, we can piece together a place of origin, the quiltmakers or participants, and the reason the quilt was made. Signature quilts are a perfect testament for women gathering together in groups for the purpose of quiltmaking. The multiplicity of signed names on one textile signifies an assembly for a common purpose. Throughout this book, I combine signature quilts with newspaper articles of group quilting. The two are a perfect alliance, with the signature quilts providing a backdrop for contemporary articles about their construction.

Not all signature quilts readily yield the clues necessary to uncover their origins and reasons for being made. Some are very helpful while others are not helpful at all. The red and green Oak Leaf and Reel Appliqué block (inscribed with Hannah M. Sheppard, Greenwich, N.J., Feb. 22nd 1847)and the Biblical quotation from Proverbs XXXI.22 ("She maketh herself coverings of tapestry") are very helpful to the researcher. The block records the person, place, time and purpose. Proverbs XXXI, which is the most quoted Biblical passage on quilts, addresses the most honored qualities of a virtuous woman.

The detail view of the Mary Silliman Chapter of the DAR quilt is a genealogical study in DAR (Daughters of the American Revolution) descendents of Revolutionary War soldiers from Bridgeport, Connecticut. Each block lists a soldier's name and at least two generations of his lineage. The appropriate National DAR Membership Number was frequently embroidered on the blocks. The Mary Silliman Chapter of the DAR Quilt is not just a signature quilt but a true genealogical record of generations of citizens from the Bridgeport area. Embroidered with red, white and blue on heavy, cream-colored silk, it was made in 1907 to be displayed at the National DAR Museum in Washington, D.C.

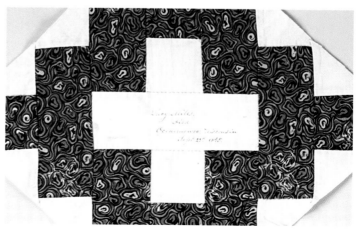

The Huron Reflector
Norwalk, Ohio
February 9, 1833

Frolics in America

When a Farmer wishes to have his corn husked, he rides round to his neighbors and informs them of his intention. An invitation of this kind was once given in my presence. The farmer entered the house, sat down, and after the customary compliments were passed, in the usual laconic style, the following dialogue took place. "I guess I'll husk my corn tomorrow afternoon" – "You've a mighty heap this year"– and the matter was arranged. All these gatherings denominate "frolics"—such as "cornhusking frolics," "apple-cutting frolic," "quilting frolic," &c. &c. ....

Newark Daily Advocate
Newark, Ohio,
April 10, 1884, page 3

A QUILTING FROLIC
Among the Colored Folks Down in Alabama
Anna P. Stow, *Kansas City Journal*

You have never attended a negro quilting. They do not refuse an invitation, for with the country negroes it is the crowning frolic of all others—if we except a colored funeral, which combines the tragic and comic until it becomes a farce. The invitations to a quilting are given out several days beforehand, and the whole neighborhood is aroused by accounts of the supper, the band, etc. Of course the time is all night after work is done, and the place of meeting one of the negro cabins.

The quilt consisting of a multiformity of pieces of worsted calico, homespun, and bed ticking, and which would rival in variety the colors of Joseph's coat, is put into a large frame. Around this the girls are seated, each having provided herself with a thimble, and the strife begins as to who shall do the most quilting. Two men stand, one at each end of the frame, holding candles, and at the back of the chair stand a chosen beau to thread the needles. It does not take long to finish the work for, of course, time is economical in the length of the stitch. When done, the girl who triumphantly takes the last stitch, becomes the belle of the evening, and the quilt is thrown over her head while she claims a kiss from a favored gemman of the party, with whom she leads the dance, and the frolic begins. The band comprises a banjo and a fiddle, and, though last, not least, patter. They always have a "patter," one who beats time by striking his knees regularly with his hands. The refreshments consist of candy, whisky and occasionally cake made of meal and molasses, served at indefinite intervals. This "quilting" continues until 2 or 3 o'clock in the morning...

"The Quilting."—Drawn by Henry Bacon, reproduced in Harper's Bazar. April 14, 1885, page 241

Denton Journal
Denton, Maryland
July 3, 1875, page 1

THE ORIGIN OF "BEE"

The term "Bee," now so generally applied to spelling classes, has for a century or more been used in connection with quiltings, corn huskings, apple butter boilings, and other pleasant gatherings of country people, where the buzy industry reminded one of the activity of a beehive. When the quilt was completed, or the corn all husked, the youngsters generally amuse themselves with dancing, playing games &c., and amongst other pleasant amusements spelling classes were introduced. To these old fashioned country customs, we think may be traced the origin of the term "bee," in its application to orthographic contest.

Stevens Point Journal
Stevens Point, Wisconsin
December 22, 1883, page 3

It is at the quilting "bee" where you hear the stinging remarks.—N.Y. News.

Marion Weekly Star
Marion, Ohio
October 10, 1885, page 6

Old fashioned quilting and husking bees are the latest church amusements. The ladies bring a quilt and do quilting, and the gentlemen are set to work over a pile of ears of corn. The girls take a hand too, but a committee examines the ears to see that there are no red ones among the pile.

Edwardsville Intelligencer
Edwardsville, Illinois
August 31, 1892, page 6

The Provincial "Bee"

A "bee" in provincial New England and New York is an assemblage of people for a set purpose, and especially a meeting of neighbors to unite in working for an individual of family. In the form of "spelling bee" or spelling match the word has extended over the whole country. Quilting bees are attended by young women, who assemble around the frame of a bed-quilt and in one afternoon accomplish more than one person could in weeks. Refreshments and beaux help to render the meeting agreeable. Apple bees are occasions where neighbors assemble to gather apples or cut them up for drying. Husking bees, for husking corn, meet in barns. In some new districts on the arrival of a new settler the neighboring farmers unite with their teams, cut the timber and build him a log house in a single day; these are termed raising bees. The name may have come from the likeness of these gatherings to the swarming of buzzing bees.

The Fort Wayne Sentinel
Fort Wayne, Indiana
January 19, 1895, page 3

The following invitations have been issued by Mrs. A. O. Waterman and Mrs. A. J. Downing for January 22 at "Sunnyside:"

Pile in on the seat
Of the runners so fleet.
All aboard for the farm,
Heigh O !
And our Quilting Bee
Will be fun, you'll see
With a merry ride
Over the snow.

"A Quilting Bee in Old Colonial Days,"
The Modern Priscilla

A Quilting Bee in Old Colonial Days

The Ohio Repository
Canton, Ohio
January 2, 1835, page 1
From the *Albany Microscope*

THE QUILTING

The day is set, the ladies met,
And at the frames are seated,
    In order placed, they work in haste,
To get the quilt completed.
    While fingers fly, their tongues they ply,
And animate their labors,
    By counting beaux, discussing clothes,
Or talking of their neighbors.
    'Dear, what a pretty frock you've on'—
'I'm very glad you like it.'
    'I'm told that Miss Micomicon
Don't speak to Mr. Micate.'
    'I saw Miss Bell the other day
Young Brown's new gig adorning'—
    'What keeps your sister Ann away?'
'She went to Troy this morning.'
    ''Tis time to roll—my needle's broke'
'So Tabor's stock is selling;
    'Abby's wedding gown's bespoke,'
'Lend me your scissors, Ellen.'
    'That match will never come about '—
'Now don't fly in a passion'—
    'Corsets, they say, are going out'
'Yet bucks are all the fashion.'
    The quilt is done, the tea begun—
The beaux are all collecting;
    The table's clear'd—the music heard,
His partner each selecting.
    The merry band, in order stand,
The dance begins with vigor—
    And rapid feet the measures beat,
And trip the mazy figure.
    Unheeded by, the moment's fly,
Old Time himself seems dancing,
    Till night a dull eye is op'd to spy—
The steps of morn advancing.
    Then closely stow'd to each abode,
The carriages go tilting,
    And many a dream has for its theme,
The pleasures of the quilting.

Waukesha Plaindealer
Waukesha, Wisconsin
June 3, 1873, page 4

A quilting party is now styled a "piece" jubilee.

The Landmark
Statesville, North Carolina
March 31, 1882, page 3

Our good housewives and fair maidens are busy at this season of the year in making up patchwork quilts. The quiltings and choppings are time honored institutions with country people. The men have the choppings and invite the neighbors in to help, and the good housewife invites her friends to help get out the quilt. Thus they mutually assist each other in their hard jobs. The merits of the various styles of quilts, the combination of figures and contrast of colors are now vigorously discussed, the Hexagon, the Octagon, Log Cabin, Album, Pride of Virginia and the Belle of Carolina all have their beauties unfolded and peculiar charms freely canvassed in the poetical style and musical voices of our fascinating ladies.

The Saturday Herald
Decatur, Illinois
April 2, 1887, page 5

Piece Congress – an old fashioned quilting party.

The Landmark
Statesville, North Carolina
July 28, 1903, page 1

Glory to the Old Quilting Party!
Monroe Enquirer

It is refreshing to read among the society notes that down (up) in Clay county they have had an old fashioned quilting and a good dinner. Now, that beats your "at homes" with a little cup of tea in one room, a piece of cake about as large as your finger in another room and then some kind of truck in a saucer in another room. An old fashioned quilting with chicken pie, garden truck of all kinds, in big dishes, big cups of coffee and all that topped off with pie and four or five story cake is not to be mentioned in the same breath with one of these "functions" where style is a plenty and eating slim. And then there is something else which makes us warm up to the quilting party. We never heard of any good women who attended one getting mad and mouthing and raising the devil because all their names was not in type as big as your hand in the local paper. Blessings on the quilting party, which same we can't say concerning some social "functions."

Floral Appliqué Quilt, dated 1846-1847, Charleston, South Carolina, Savannah and Macon, Georgia. Hand pieced, hand appliquéd, hand quilted, 111 inches x 107 inches, cotton. This quilt was handed down as a wedding quilt, although there is no strong provenance to support the purpose for this quilt. The Prussian Blue prints in this quilt make it shine.

CHAPTER 2

"The Pleasures of the "Quilting!"

QUILTMAKING AND COURTING

THE QUILTING PARTY.

As Sung By R. H. Racey. — Air : *Betsy Baker*.

It was down at Major Parson's house,
    The gals they had a quilting,
Just for to show their handsome looks,
    And have a little jilting.
There was Deacon Parson's daughter Sal,
    Squire Wheeler's daughter Mary,
And General Carter's youngest gal
    That looked just like a Fairy.

There was Lucy White and Martha Brown,
    And Jackson's daughter Betty,
Femimo Pinkhorn, Prudence Short,
    And Major Downing's Hetty.
But if there was a handsome gal
    That would make a feller's heart right,
I guess it was, by all accounts,
    Miss Carolina Cartright.

O, as they were a whirling plate,
    And playing hunt the slipper,
Jerusha Parson's went to git
    Some cider in the dipper ;
But just as she had left the room,
    And got into the entry
She gave a scream and stood stock-still,
    Just like a frozen sentry.

We all run out, and there, I swow,
    Both huggin' like creation :
Miss Cartright and Sam Jones we saw
    A kissing like a tarnation.
O, such a laugh as we sat up,
    You never heerd a finer.
Says I, I reckon kissing's cheap,
    Don't you Miss Carolina ?

You ought to see Miss Cartright blush,
    Just as if she'd fainted ;
She said she had the toothache,
    And in Samuel's arms had fainted.
Now, all young gals, I'll say to you :
    When you go to a quilt-make,
Don't let the fellers hug and kiss,
    Unless you've got the toothache.

H. DE MARSAN, Successor to J. ANDREWS, Publisher, dealer in songs and Toy Books, Paper Dolls &c., 38 Chatham Street, N. Y.

The Eliza Hager Quilt, dated 1843-44, New Brunswick and Newark, New Jersey. Hand pieced, hand quilted, 94 inches x 94 inches, cotton. Much thought went into the making of this unusual, early signature quilt. The block was intricately pieced with components of three different styles of quilt blocks including: Delectable Mountains and Eight-Point Stars. Eliza Hager's name is featured in the center block with a double, Eight-Point Star. The quilt is bound with woven tape. *Collection of Judy Grow.*

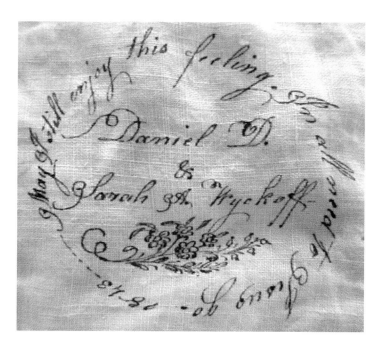

Watertown Chronicle
Watertown, Wisconsin
February 14, 1849, page 1

The Quilting Party

Reader! Were you ever at a quilting party —an old fashioned quilting party? If not, you will do well to read our description, which of course falls far short of the realty; and this reality, as the thing is now nearly obsolete, you may never have the satisfaction of witnessing. 'Tis one of the pleasantest things in the whole round of a country life to attend one of these gatherings-together of the young and light-hearted. Let it be understood in the first place that these quiltings are indispensible. The quilts, &c., must be made; the girls must have their "things ready" as the phrase is; or they will assuredly meet with no attention from the marriage-seeking young men. The preparation of the requisites of domestic life is a sort of implied declaration of readiness to receive the address of the lover, and to encounter the perils of matrimony, and is understood and acted upon accordingly.

When the quilting is to take place, the respectable young ladies of the neighborhood are all invited: there is no aristocracy; no singling out of favored individuals. They assemble early at the dwelling of their friend, and immediately fall to work, as if their very lives depend upon their exertions. They consider it absolutely necessary to forward their work in such a manner as to prevent any material encroachment upon the hilarity and mirth of the evening. The evening is looked forward to with a great deal of satisfaction, and many a fine eye glances impatiently as the slowly setting sun, whose tardiness seems to mock the feverish anticipations of the fair quilters.

Night at length comes: a New England winter night—for the quiltings are usually in the long evenings of the winter—with skins, clear, beautifully clear, in the dark coloring of the sky, moonlight resting like a smile upon the white luster of the snow, streaming through the naked branches of the wild forest trees, and flushing like pale fires upon the distant icy hills. The merry sound of bells now rings upon the ears of the fair listeners within doors.

"The fellows are coming," cries some eager voice, and a sudden smile steals like electricity around the apartment. There is a moment of rapid preparation, a hasty glance at the small mirror, a trembling adjustment of curls and combs—and then all are seated demurely at work. One after another the "fellows" arrive, until the apartment is literally crowded with as merry a company as ever laughed away an evening. The girls however, remain perseveringly at their work, their hands stooping almost to the outstretched quilt before them, now and then exchanging a sly glance, or a smart reply or a meaning nod, with the fine, healthy looking gentlemen around them. They are soon interrupted, and one complains of the loss of her thimble, another that her thread has been taken away, and another that the "fellows plague her so that she won't work or touch to," and in a few moments Babel-like confusion is effected, very much to the satisfaction of all parties. The owner of the quilt now interferes, and carefully removes the quilting frame, blushing all the while at the good natured jokes of the young men relative to herself, her quilt, and lover, who—if she is so fortunate as to have one—is pretty sure to be present. The scene is now all life and gaiety. In one part of the room may be seen the student of the old village Doctor, amusing and astonishing by his quotations of Latin—and laughing at the amazement of his friends. Hard by is the schoolmaster of the district, a privileged and favored personage, you may know him by his pale cheek and fair hands. He is leaning familiarly over the chair of a pretty girl, the fairest in the room. She is telling his fortune by the old and curious method of palmistry, tracing out with her own pretty fingers the lines of good and bad fortune which intersects the hand of the master.—

There are strange blushes on her cheek, and they steal at times even to her neck, with a variable and beautiful play of coloring.— She knows that the eye of the general favorite is upon her, and her young heart thrilling with a new sense of joy. Nor will her pleasant dream be broken in upon by disappointment. There is honest love, but nothing of the deceitful and designing in gaze of her lover.

The Mountain Democrat
Placerville, California
June 16, 1855, page 2

When I saw Sweet Nelly Home
By Mary Francis Kyle

Our readers will agree with us that the following lines are very fine—equally tender in sentiment and melodious in rhythm:

In the sky the bright stars glittered,
On the grass the moonlight fell,
Hushed the sound of daylight's bustle,
Closed the "Pink eyed pimpernel"
As down the moss grown wood-pitch—
Where the cattle love to roam—
From aunt Pattie's quilting party
I was seeing Nelly home.

Jetty ringlets safely fluttered
O'er a brow as white as snow;
And her cheek!—the crimson sunset
Scarcely has a winter glow.
'Mid her parted lips' vermillion
White teeth flushed like ocean foam,
All I marked with pulses throbbing,
While I saw sweet Nelly home.

When the Autumn tinged the greenwood
Turning all its leaves to gold,
In the lawn, by alders shaded,
I my love to Nelly told.
As we stood together, gazing
On the star bespangled dome,
How I blest the August evening
When I saw sweet Nelly home.

White hairs mingle with my tresses,
Furrows steal upon my brow,
But a love smile cheers and blesses
Life's declining moments now;
Matron in the snowy 'kerchief,
Closer to my bosom come—
Tell me, dost thou still remember
When I saw sweet Nelly home?
—From *The Boston Post*

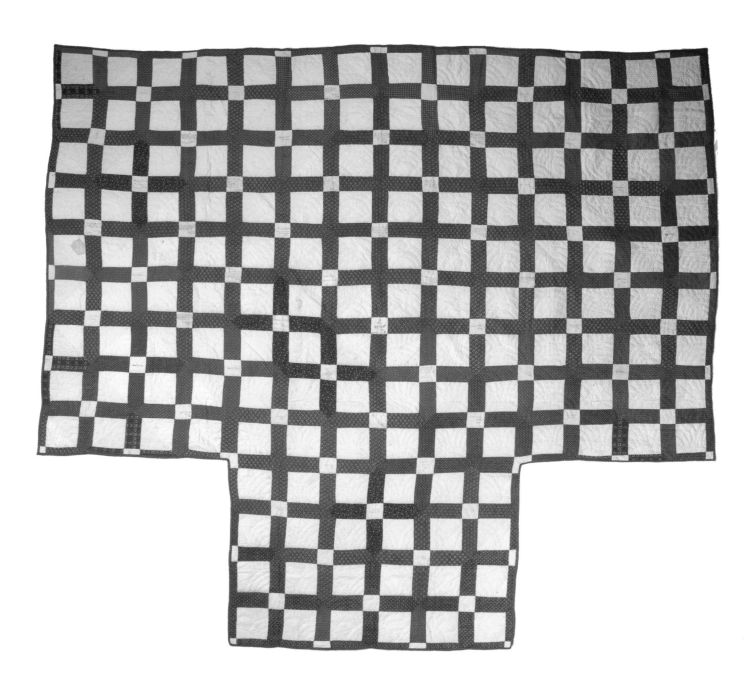

Snowflake Signature Quilt, Salisbury, Massachusetts, dated May – July, 1851, hand pieced, hand quilted, 108 inches x 98 inches, cotton. Inscriptions and signatures suggest the quilt was made for a member of the community who was leaving the area to marry. The quilt was made with samples of multiple Turkey Red prints commonly seen in the mid-nineteenth century.

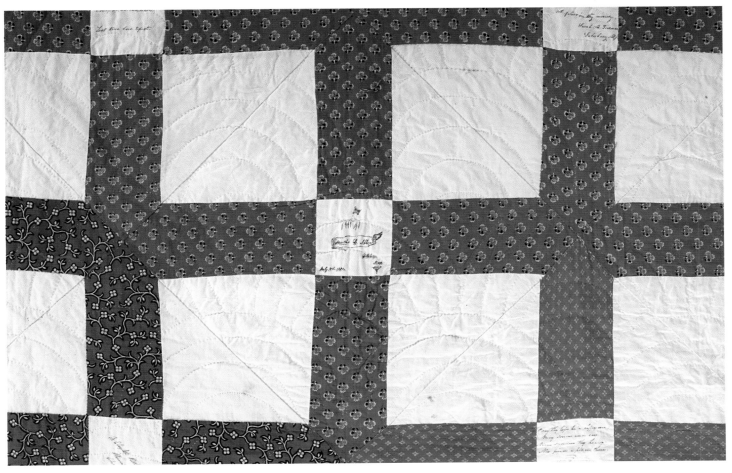

Republican Compiler
Gettysburg, Pennsylvania
June 9, 1856, page 1

Mr. Bates met Sally Jones for the first time at the quilting, and in sixty seconds after sight he had determined to court her. He sat beside her as she stitched, and even had the audacity to squeeze her hand under the quilt. Truth is mighty and must be told.— Although Sally did not resent the impertinence by a stick with her needle, she was not half so indignant as she ought to have been. I dare not say she was pleased, but perhaps I should not be far from the truth if I did. It is undeniable the more gentle and modest a woman is, the more she admires courage and boldness in the other sex....

Chester Times
Chester, Pennsylvania
December 10, 1883, page 12

Batchelors at a Quilting Party

Trenton, N.J., Dec. 10 – Preparatory to a fair to be given by the Warren Street Methodist Church in this city, twelve batchelors of the congregation were induced by the ladies to agree to furnish a quilt of their own making. Thursday evening was fixed as the time for the quilting bee, and an admission fee of ten cents was charged. The batchelors surrounded the quilting frame and worked conscientiously with needles and thread for several hours until the ladies came to their relief and helped complete the quilt. The quilt is said to be a triumph of art. It is composed of sunflowers, old maids, batchelors, baskets, and other quilt combinations, and will be offered for sale at the fair. Among the bachelor quilters were a railroad man, a printer, two brick manufacturers, and no tailor.

Daily Gazette
Fort Wayne, Indiana
September 4, 1884, page 6

Quilting parties are raging in the west end. Last night a dozen pretty misses surrounded a frame and with nimble fingers traced the designs, which beautified the necessary article of comfort.

Morning Oregonian
Portland, Oregon
December 8, 1884, page 13

It was the day of Mrs. Larcom's quilting, and supper was almost ready. The quilt was already out, and by a little preconcerted maneuver on the part of the fun-loving girls, it had been thrown over the widow's head, when taken out of the frame, a piece of mischief which afforded no little amusement, as, according to time-honored tradition, whoever the quilt is first thrown over is soon to become a bride.

Mrs. Blossom wore her honors blushingly, and her cheeks were still covered with crimson when the gentlemen began to drop in just before supper.

Lawyer Greene, who was among the first to arrive, was profuse in his attentions to the blooming widow, much to the discomfiture of his less fortunate rival, who could only sit in a corner and cast despairing glances at the object of his affections.

Marion Daily Star
Marion, Ohio
April 7, 1885, page 1

A Georgia Quilting

A quilting was organized at the house of a very bashful young man by the young ladies of this settlement, with a view of getting him into society. The day being arranged and everything in readiness, the girls met and commenced the fun. The young man thought, to evade the crowd, he would go to the back side of the plantation to work, and he took himself thither and commenced operations in a secluded spot. He had not been there long before he encountered a huge coach-whip snake which made fight. The young man had to hit the grit lively. He started homeward and the snake after him. As he moved he looked back over his shoulder occasionally, but his snakeship was there. He opened his throttle and got up railroad speed, and at last reached the yard fence exhausted. He fell into the yard, when one of the girls rescued him and killed the snake. The snake had struck at him and fastened its fangs into his coat so it could not get it loose until he reached home. —Moral: Young man, don't be bashful, not too much so.

Jackson (Ga.) Argus

Mitchell Daily Republican
Mitchell, South Dakota
July 1, 1886, page 4

It is entirely unfair for a man to sneer at a woman's inability to understand a baseball game until he has proven his own ability to grapple with the mysteries of a crazy quilt social.

—*Fall River Advance*

Trenton Times
Trenton, New Jersey
January 15, 1887, page 4

She who takes the last stitch at a quilting will be the first to marry.

"Square in a Square" Signature Quilt, dated 1883, Essex, Connecticut, hand pieced, hand and machine assembled, 75 inches x 100 inches, cotton. The families of the signers on this quilt lived across Long Island Sound from one another in Essex, Connecticut and Mattituck, Long Island, New York. The distant was just a short boat ride. The travel time by land would have taken one or two days in 1883.

25

Herald & Torch Light
Haegerstown, Maryland
April 11, 1889, page 1

One winter by the Merrimac, some two-
score years ago,
You could not see the fence-rails for the
drifted heaps of snow;
The flocks of chickadees would come and
in the door-yard stand,
Too hunger-tamed to fear the touch of e'em
a boyish hand,
I sat beside the kitchen fire; the chores at
last were done;
The farmer's wife, unwilling, owned my
tasks a rest had won.
When down the road, all silver-sweet, the
sleigh bells jingle came,
And through the frosty air I heard, thrice
called in haste, my name;
Imperious a girlish voice: "Oh! John, be
quick, for see,
You're wanted over at the Spragues! They've
got a quiltin' bee."
A quilting bee." I held my breath. "And pray,
what good are you?"
I heeded not the dame's sharp tongue, she
always was a shrew;
But coat and muffler hurried on, I sprang
into the sleigh.
And like the wind we flew along behind the
Squire's old bay.
A little hand stole into mine, a low laugh
rippled fleet.
And mixed its music with the chimes so
rollicking and sweet;
Perhaps – perhaps – I kissed her cheek, the
merry blue-eyed maid,
Perhaps we whispered loving words, but
pace we never staid
Till at the Spragues' our rein we drew, and
saucy Kate to me
Said airily, "I've brought you, John, to Sally's
Quiltin' bee."
The house was gay with candlelight, the
lamps were all aglow,
The ruddy flame came streaming forth
across the shining snow,
The girls were sitting by the frame, their
needles out and in
Went flashing, flashing to and fro, through
such a merry din,
You could scarcely hear yourself for fun,
and when the work was o'er,
Then swift we piled away the chairs, and
cleared the kitchen floor,
And Uncle Archie drew his bow across the
fiddle strings,
And men and maids, we danced that night
as if our feet were wings.
My word! the very thought of that sets this
old heart a thrill,

I'd dance again as then I danced, and with
a right good will,
If Kate could call me once again, as sweet
as sweet could be,
"Come, John, make haste, you're wanted,
John, at Sally's quiltin' bee."
But Kate, my Kate, for many a year, no
mortal ears have heard
The tones which rang with melody,
surpassing any birds;
The angels wanted her too soon; they always
want the best;
They take the one whose absence leaves an
ache in every breast.
Her grave is in the open ground, beneath
the open sky,
Right in the fair home meadow, where her
father's people lie;
And I have been a lonely man, and cumbered
oft with care.
And bowed beneath the burden that my
darling used to share.
I little thought how soon the golden to
ashen gray would be
Turned darkly, when I went with Kate to
Sally's quilting-bee.
What's that, young man? You've come to say
that you and daughter Sue
Would like to join your hands for life – that
shehas promised you,
In case her father will consent. "He will, the
dear old dad,"
She cries, and 'tis the same sweet way her
darling mother had.
And she, though not a touch to Kate, has
dancing eyes of blue,
And cheeks that hide the dimples, where the
bluish comes peeping through.
Take her, young man, be good to her; if I
have had my day,
I'll not begrudge the happiness that seems
to point that way.
But much I doubt if you will know the bliss
that fell to me,
When Kate said "yes" that night we went to
Sally's quilting-bee.

Daily Kennebec Journal
Augusta, Maine
November 8, 1900

Autumn in Maine

Evenings cool ye spelling school,
And quilting bees have come;
Moonlight rides with would-be brides,
And sewing circles hum.
Apple treat, with cider sweet,
Lads and lasses hearty,
Dances, whirls and kissing girls.
At the surprise party.
Big logs grace the fireplace,
Sports will bring forth joy;
Offer a dish, now don't you wish
You were a farmer's boy?

Hopewell Herald
Hopewell, New Jersey
January 23, 1901, page 3

There seem to be quite a number of quilting
parties in this vicinity at present. Someone has
said that weddings are sure to follow parties of
this kind. Whether this be true or not we do not
pretend to say, but we do know that some quilts
that we have seen are certainly beautiful—almost
as beautiful as the fair ones to whom they
belong.

The Landmark
Statesville, North Carolina
February 7, 1902, page 11

A couple dashing young men of
Statesville will learn with regret that
pretty Miss Kate Clark, of Longford,
is to be an old maid. She attended
a quilting at Mrs. Wagner's yesterday and there is an old saying (which
must be infallible) that if a girl has
a newly-made quilt thrown over her
head, though she struggled valiantly
against it. That settles it and she's
no longer on the carpet.

Chimney Sweep/Album Signature Quilt, c. 1840, Cherry Valley/Westford/Duanesburg/Otsego County, New York. Hand pieced, hand quilted, 84 inches x 92 inches, cotton. This quilt was made with some beautiful Prussian Blue prints. It is an excellent example of the variety of fabrics available to quiltmakers around 1840.

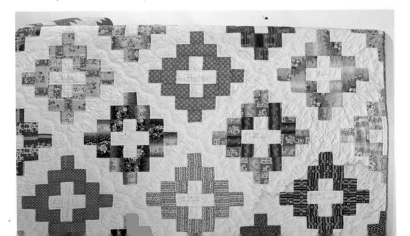

Chimney Sweep/Album Signature Quilt, c.1840, Portland and Middletown, Connecticut; Windsor, Vermont, hand pieced, hand quilted, 79 inches x 80 inches, cotton. The fabrics in this quilt reflect the variety of beautiful fabrics in the mid-1840s.

Nine Patch Diamond Quilt, dated 1844, hand pieced, machine assembled, hand tied, 84 inches x 98.5 inches, cotton. The tied quilt is signed with the names of the members and friends of the Flanders family from Grafton, Sharon, Boscawen, and Gifford, New Hampshire, and Stafford and Pomfret, Vermont. Research Sources: 1840 and 1850 United States Censuses.

Chimney Sweep Quilt Top, dated 1861, Michigan, hand pieced, 86 inches x 100 inches, cotton. The most common family names inscribed on this quilt are Howland, Colvin, Griswold, McNeill, and Dowling. The Michigan counties represented are Washtenaw, Lenawee, and Jackson County.

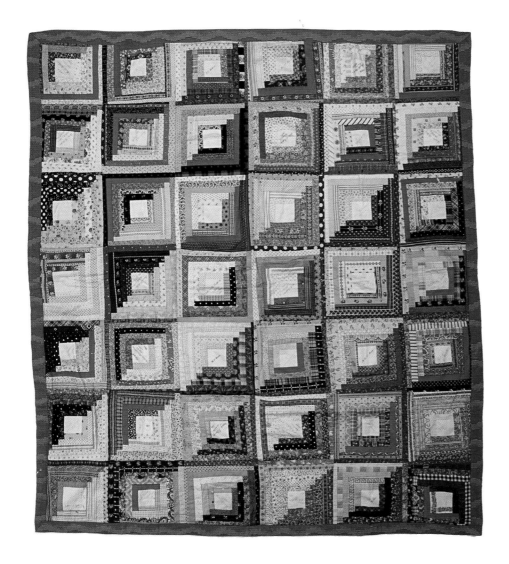

Log Cabin Signature Quilt, dated 1882, Waterbury, Connecticut, hand pieced, 55 inches x 63 inches, cotton. Signature quilts come in every imaginable pattern, however, Log Cabin signature quilts are rarely seen.

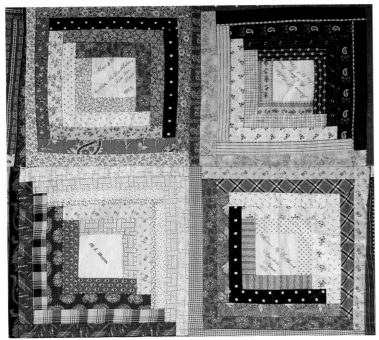

Gazette Bulletin
Williamsport, Pennsylvania
September 13, 1876

A Quilting Bee Last Night

Lower Vine street was the scene of an old fashioned quilting party last night, and the neighborly matrons congregated in force to assist in the worthy enterprise. The tri-colored patches were arranged in order to produce the most striking effect, and the needles were plied vigorously, in the olden time, however, it was customary to chalk a string and snap it across the quilt to insure straight lines, and not infrequently a kettle of apple butter would be swinging on the kitchen crane. But, although these features were omitted in this instance, fun and frolic reigned supreme, and the ladies, refreshed with good sweet cider and hearty repast, were unanimous in proclaiming their fair hostess a Trump.

Denton Journal
Denton, Kansas
June 19, 1880

Quilting bees are going out of fashion. The women who can sew are dying of old age.

Stevens Point Journal
Stevens Point, Wisconsin
April 9, 1881

A Ladies' luncheon is described as the luxurious daughter of the old-fashioned quilting party.

Dover Weekly Argus
Canal Dover, Ohio
January 6, 1882

A quilting party of the style of one hundred years ago was held at the residence of the Governor of Kentucky the other evening, nearly all the members of the Legislature being present. On the tables were cold 'possum, pop-corn, apple toddy and pumpkin pie.

The Globe
Atchison, Kansas
January 7, 1882

At a thousand guest "quilting" party given Governor and Mrs. Blackburn, of Kentucky, last week, Mr. Graham, of Louisville, at the age of 98, danced reels and jigs and cut "pigeon wings" in the most admirable and astonishing manner.

He had not danced before in thirty years, but thinks to recover his former skill by the time he gets to be 100 or 110 years of age.

Stevens Point Journal
Stevens Point, Wisconsin
December 15, 1882

We will not forget the quilting at Mrs. Leslie Strong's last Friday. There were a goodly number of young and a few married ladies in attendance. M. W. Rice was there a short time and left his mark of his work on the quilt, soon left the ladies to their own destruction and went home. In the evening the young were gathered in and all enjoyed a few hours pleasantly chatting, reading and singing. All returned home pronouncing the entertainment fine.

Reno Evening Gazette
Reno, Nevada
February 15, 1883

Cat Shaking
—New York Sun
Kentucky is indulging in quilting bees and cat shaking. After the quilting a cat is put upon the quilt. The young folks take hold of the corners and toss the animal until it jumps off upon one of the young ladies, who is then crowned queen of the bee.

Stevens Point Journal
Stevens Point, Wisconsin
December 22, 1883

The quilting party at Mrs. Henry Heasslers was a success. The ladies finished quilting the quilt and got it nearly bound. The party in the evening, well, we have heard so much about it we will forebear giving it publicity. Those acquainted with the circumstances, know enough to satisfy themselves and what might be told your readers would do them no good.

Evening Observer
Dunkirk, New York
May 2, 1884

A new game called cat shaking has been instituted at quilting frolics in the country, it is said. After the quilting a cat is put upon the quilt. The young folks take hold of the corners and toss the animal till it jumps off upon one of the young ladies who is crowned queen of the bee. It is considered great fun for everyone except the cat.

GOING TO THE SEWING SOCIETY WITH **WILLIMANTIC** THREAD.

THE HATCH LITH CO NEW YORK

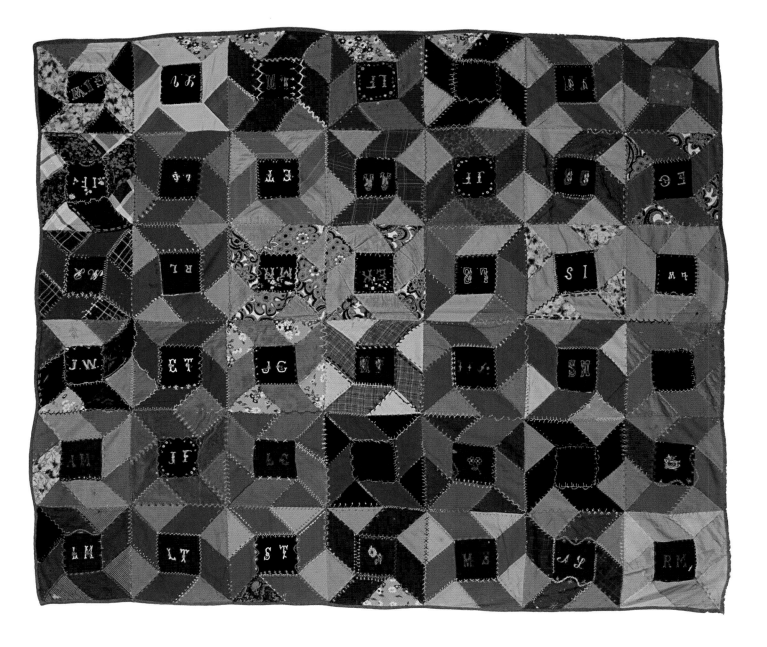

Eccentric Star Quilt. (Brackman) Foundation pieced by hand, hand embroidered, 74 inches x 85 inches, velvet and silk. This friendship quilt was embroidered with initials in many beautiful fonts. Each set of initials is further embellished with floral designs.

Daily Gazette
Fort Wayne, Indiana
September 4, 1884

Quilting Parties are raging in the west end. Last night a dozen pretty misses surrounded a frame and with nimble fingers traced the designs, which beautified the necessary article of comfort.

The Landmark
Statesville, North Carolina
November 22, 1888, page 1

A Bear at a Quilting Bee

A few days ago there was a quilting bee at the house of John Holliday, who occupies a hut built on a lean-to against a cliff among the mountains, near Greenwood, Ky. Here is an account of the affair:

Quilting bees are great occasions in the mountains, and all the women within a radius of fifteen miles usually gather at them. This was a big one. Mrs. Holliday's hospitality was renowned throughout her section. The two older children -- boys aged 11 and 9 – were off at work with their father. little low upper room under the roof, reached by a ladder. There they amused themselves as best they could, while about thirty women congregated around the quilting frame below, and labored assiduously at sewing and exchanging the news of the neighborhood. Mrs. Holliday made frequent trips to the little kitchen where a savory dinner was preparing.

It lacked about an hour of noon, The conversation of the "quilters" had become very lively, and their laughter could be heard to the edge of the clearing. Then there was a heavy thump overhead. "What's that !" exclaimed one of the women.

"Only one of them children tumbled over on the floor above," said Mrs. Holliday, "you needn't mind'em."

Probably they would have continued their quilting, but "them children" began to scream, and one after another they came tumbling down the ladder. The last was the youngest – a little girl. She was only four years old, and she did "tumble down," falling through the trap door to the floor, but she was so fat that the fall didn't hurt her.

She failed to bring with her the larger part of her pinafore, but her mother didn't have time to notice that, for the next moment a big black bear popped through the opening right after the children. He turned a somersault as he fell, but he held in his claws the missing portion of the baby's pinafore.

Some of the women screamed and rushed for the door. These were the younger ones. The older had steadier nerves. They had lived in the mountains all their lives; they had seen bears before. The children were seized by them, while Mrs. Holliday ran to the smoke house, where her husband had left his rifle that morning after cleaning it out.

Somebody might have been hurt, but the bear was slightly stunned by his precipitous descent, and when he recovered consciousness nobody was within easy reach. The savory smell of the cooking dinner attracted him, and he pushed his way into the little kitchen. A piece of fat mutton was boiling in a kettle over the fire place, for Mrs. Holliday had not yet bought a stove. Bruin made for it, and burnt his nose. While he was growling and rubbing his paws over his nose Mrs. Holliday poked the rifle through the window, and shot him dead.

The bear had been wandering along the cliff above the house. His explorations led him near the edge and he lost his footing and tumbled over and struck on the cabin roof below. The light boards gave way and he fell right into the group of children. They scattered, and the bear following them, tumbled down the ladder, which serving as a stairway. He was the first bear seen this season in this part of Kentucky, and weighed nearly 400 pounds.

Though he had arrived suddenly, and in a manner somewhat unwelcome, the bear did not permanently break up the quilting. The guests were quickly gathered together again. Mr. Holliday came up a few minutes later, it being his dinner hour. Skilful hands assisted him, the bear was skinned, and some of his choicest steaks graced the dinner Mrs. Holliday spread at her quilting.

The Landmark
Statesville, North Carolina
July 4, 1889, page 4

Tricks of a Coon

Most animals seem capable of proving responsive to petting, though some may become embarrassing associates on close acquaintance. A Southern man who had a pet coon tells in the Atlanta Constitution some entertaining tales of that animal. He says: "Once carried the coon with me to a quilting at a place where there was a swarm of bees. You know a coon loves honey better than anything. The quilting was proceeding nicely — all the womenfolks sitting around plying their needles — when in dashed the coon, literally covered with bees. He rushed under the quilt, strewing the mad insects. I tell you the quilting moved, and the chairs flew, and the dresses flapped and such a dancing was never seen before. Pet coons were not worth much in that market afterward.

Freeborn County Standard
Albert Lea, Minnesota
September 12, 1889 page 8

There was a basket picnic in Mrs. Buchanan's grove last Saturday afternoon gotten up for the little girls who had been organized into a band called The Jewel Workers. They succeeded in getting up a quilt for Mrs. Hammond of a beautiful design, the blocks are of white muslin worked by red thread, the names of persons giving 10 cents towards it are worked on the quilt with leaves of different kinds; this with $12 in money were given to Mrs. Hammond, it being a surprise to her. The rest of the afternoon was spent in select reading, music and singing, social visiting, and ending with a grand supper which the ladies had prepared. Everybody seemed to enjoy themselves well.

The News
Frederick, Maryland
February 27, 1894

COUNTY CORRESPONDENCE

A Consensus of Current Events in County Towns—BEAVER DAM—FEB. 26

This valet takes the lead in quilting bees this spring. Scarcely a week passes but what there is a social gathering at some neighbor's home. This week it was at Richard Boone's, where the workers found two quilts in frame awaiting them, the married ladies taking charge of one and the single ones the other. While the former did the most work, the latter made up for lost time in chatter and giggle. Your correspondent appeared on the scene in time to get a good supply of mince pie that would have been credit to Mary Jane.

Indiana Progress
Indiana, Pennsylvania
January 16, 1896

A "QUILTIN' " PARTY

An old fashioned "quiltin" party was held in Third ward Thursday. Twelve of the near neighbors of Mrs. L. M. White gathered at her home that day. This "quiltin" party made haps, and when evening came the fifth one was taken from the frames. Mrs. White served a delicious supper to her friends and the event ended pleasantly.

Evening Herald
Syracuse, New York
November 7, 1899

"The Quilting Party," taken from the social life of Madison county in 1825, was the fourth scene. In this the younger generations saw things as they have been described of their grandmothers. The old women talked about their neighbors, took snuff and had a perfectly lovely time while they "tied off the quilt." The hostess was Mrs. William W. Warr, and among the guests was Mrs. Boll D. Moot, whose gown was the one that she wore on her wedding day—forty-two years ago. Assessor Jacob Winnie had just got interested in cracking nuts for the children, when the place was taken possession of by young people of the dancing age and everything else was suspended to give them the floor.

Coshocton Age
Coshocton, Ohio
April 24, 1900

A quilting bee and hum social at Mrs. S. E. Lee's was attended by many ladies Thursday.

Stereoscope cards were popular in the fourth quarter of the nineteenth century. This card features little girls and their quilting party.

"Housewives in Tygart Valley, West Virginia, have weekly group meetings in home economics. Here they are quilting." 1938, LC-USF34-050077-E, Library of Congress Prints and Photographs Division Washington, D.C.

Apron Signature Quilt Top, machine pieced, hand appliquéd, 70 inches x 72 inches, cotton.

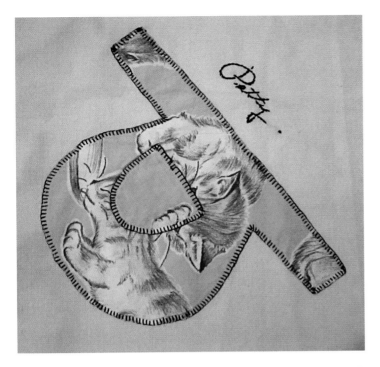

"Quilting in sharecropper's home near Pace, Mississippi. Background photo for Sunflower Plantation." LC-USZ62-129821, Library of Congress Prints & Photographs Division Washington, D.C.

"Farm women working on quilt." Near West Carlton, Yamhill County, Oregon." LC-USF34- 021150-E, Library of Congress Prints and Photographs Division Washington, DC.

This is a photo of everybody's grandparents from the 1940s-1950s. Grandma always had her apron on.

Cottage Tulip Signature Quilt, c. 1935, Colville, Arkansas, hand and machine pieced, hand embroidered, hand quilted, 58 inches x 81 inches, cotton. The "Cottage Tulips" pattern was published by three designers in the second quarter of the 20th Century; Evelyn Brown, Kansas City Star, and Carrie Hall. This design is rarely found as a signature quilt. The signers on this quilt are featured in the 1930 Census as farmers' wives.

Gastonia Daily Gazette
Gastonia, North Carolina
March 12, 1927

Quilting Bee

Pricked fingers, sore ribs and stiff shoulders were among the after effect of the big quilting bee at the home of Mr. and Mrs. Charley Clemmer Thursday. No regrets, however, were heard as the jolly good time together and oceans of laughter well repay. Jokes and puns vied with thread and scissors in passing over the big quilt from one side to the other.

A sumptuous dinner was served at the noon hour when the workers proved their skill also in the art of feasting.

Two large quilts were completed and another put into the frames as a result of the day together. Personnel of this quilting team were Mesdames C. W. Lineberger, M. H. Rhodes, J. A. Lingerfelt, C. I. White and sisters, of Bank Street Mrs. I. A. Rhyne, of Dallas route two, sister and Mrs. Mervin Cemmer, of South Dallas, sister-in-law of the hostess, Misses Dora Friday and Lucille Pasour.

Ladies of the Helping Hand Society working on a quilt. Gage County, Nebraska LC-USF34- 008655-D, Library of Congress Prints and Photographs Division Washington, D.C.

Sunbonnet Sue Signature Quilt, c. 1930, hand pieced, hand appliquéed, hand embroidered, 76 inches x 90 inches, cotton. With only first names inscribed upon this quilt, researching the origin of the quilt is impossible.

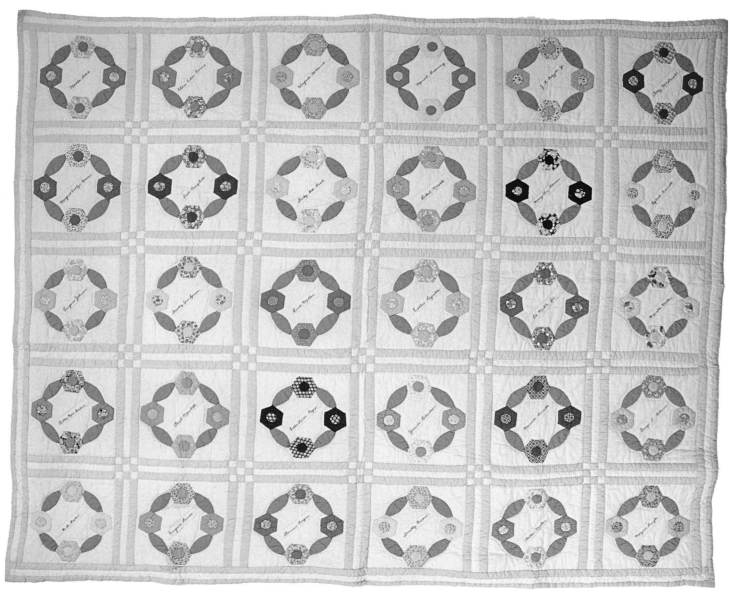

Hexagon Flower Wreath Quilt, c 1935, possibly Connecticut or New York, hand appliquéd, hand pieced, hand quilted, 70 inches x 82 inches, cotton.

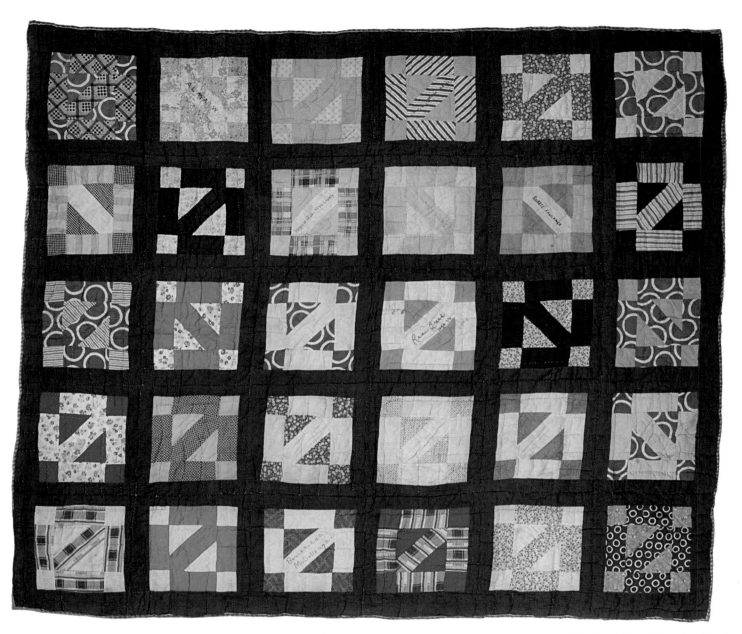

Alabama Signature Quilt, 1935, Roanoke, Randolph County, Alabama, hand and machine pieced, hand embroidered, hand quilted, cotton. "Resa Breed 16" is the key name. It assisted most in identifying the year the quilt was made and its place of origin. According to the 1930 Census record, Resa's father, Cartie Breed, was a quiller in a cotton mill and her brother was a weaver in the mill. Other names inscribed on the quilt also had relatives who worked in the cotton mill. Robbie Faulkner, signer on the quilt, was a twister in the mill.

Lima News
Lima, Ohio
February 4, 1938 , page 20

Mrs. R. C. Acton, 506 Holmes ave, entertained members of the Flower Garden QuiltCclub in her home Wednesday afternoon. Valentine decorations were carried out in the lunch served at the close of the afternoon.

"Making a quilt in Scranton, Iowa, home. The ladies will give the quilt to a needy family." LC-USF34- 060706-D, Library of Congress Prints & Photographs Division Washington, D.C.

Oshkosh Daily
Northwestern
Oshkosh, Wisconsin
September 25, 1953, page 12

Plan Quilting Bee

Hem 'n Haw Sewing club met Wednesday evening at the home of Miss Sallyjoe Otto and members discussed plans for a quilting bee. The next meeting will be held Oct. 8 at the home of Miss Amber Schmidt, 360 Broad St. Refreshments were served at the conclusion of the meeting.

Pot-of-Tulips Quilt, dated 1939, Seymour Family Signature Quilt, Springfield, Missouri, hand appliquéd, hand embroidered, hand pieced, 82 inches x 98 inches, cotton. The ground of this quilt is tan instead of the traditional color white. The green and lavender fabrics glow against this background.

Sampler Floral Appliqué Quilt, c.1950, Rapid City, South Dakota, machine pieced, hand appliquéd, hand embroidered, hand quilted, 72 inches x 72 inches, cotton.

Chain Link variation, dated 1956, and Christmas are embroidered on a block, machine pieced, hand quilted, cotton.

Cedar Point Anniversary Quilt, 1970, Cedar Point, Ohio. This quilt was painted with the names of food service workers at the famous amusement park in Sandusky, Ohio, called Cedar Point. The quilt was made in celebration of the One Hundredth Anniversary of our nation's first amusement park. The Coral Room constructed on the grounds of the spot of the Grand Pavilion built in 1888.

Shoofly Quilt, dated 1978, made for the 25th Anniversary of Theresa and Edmund Jesiolowski. Edmund is listed in the Social Security Death Index as last living in Bethlehem, Pennsylvania. The corner of the quilt is inscribed with the family of Theresa and Edmund.

75

CHAPTER 4

"His or Her Name Engraved on a Patch"
QUILTMAKING FOR A CAUSE

This late nineteenth century Puck print accurately illustrates the new focus on social awareness of the modern American girl.

Janesville Gazette
Janesville, Wisconsin
June 12, 1851

Woman's Rights Convention—A number of female celebrities held a convention at Akron, Ohio, last week. The usual resolutions were passed unanimously. The chief difficulty, however, arose in deciding who should have the floor. Of course, that would be the chief difficulty.

It should be so arranged that all can talk at once, as they do at quiltings. If it did not tend much to education, at least it would be a great economy in time, and promote woman's rights just as well. —*Chicago Jour*

"THEY MENDED AWAY THROUGH THE SUMMER DAY."

"Mending the Old Flag" illustrated in Farm Ballads by Will Carleton, Harper & Brothers, Publisher, New York 1873, Page 157.

Davenport Daily Gazette
Davenport, Iowa
December 30, 1861, page 2
and *Berkshire County Eagle*
Pittsfield, Massachusetts
January 2, 1862, page 1

The ladies of Franklin, Norfolk County, Mass, by general consent, brought together their old dresses, such as Dame Fashion had discarded, and the whole were made into fifty-six bed quilts for the soldiers. The quilting lasted for three days, in the town hall, and during a portion of the time seventy-five ladies were plying their busy needles.

Reno Evening Gazette
Reno, Nevada
July 13, 1882

Acknowledgment

Rev. and Mrs. A.B. Palmer gratefully acknowledge the receipt of $51 and a beautiful quilt as a present from their many friends. If they may reckon among their friends in Reno all whose names are recorded on this quilt they consider themselves highly favored. Such gatherings, without presents, are always in order at their home.

A movement in WILLIMANTIC Thread.

Austin Daily Herald
Austin, Minnesota
April 5, 1897, page 2

A Unique Quilt

The ladies of the Universalist Society have just completed a novel and unique piece of handiwork in the shape of a counterpane of quilt that is really a curiosity. The material is half bleached muslin outlined in red cotton. On each block there us some particular design representing some industry or organization and ingeniously interwoven are the names of the interested parties. "Grandma's fan" is a pretty block, names of the G.A.R. are clustered around a stack of musketry, the commercial travelers have an exhibit of their well worn grip, while a crowd of names on another block indicate the business men of Austin. One border gives the historical data of the society, the other border trills a lullaby of our childhood days. To see it is to appreciate the value of it. It will be placed on exhibition this week for a day or two in some window on Main street, where the friends can examine it and estimate its value and at the annual supper with hot fritters and maple sugar it will be offered for sale, when they will have an opportunity to bid it in and hold it as their own.

Eau Claire Leader
Eau Claire, Wisconsin
July 13, 1899, page 13

Woman's Relief Corp is now selling tickets on a quilt for the benefit of the New Richmond sufferers, and it is hoped hat all will buy a ticket when called upon, and help this most worthy cause along.

Newport Mercury
Newport, Rhode Island
December 2, 1882, page 1

Announcing the Returns

The Ladies' Relief Association of the Union Congregational Church, assisted by the Union Progressive Literary association will give a literary and social entertainment in the church next Thursday at 8 o'clock. At this time the votes will be counted that have been cast for the pastors of the Union, Shiloh and Touro Chapel churches for the autograph quilt containing the autographs of many hundreds living in several States. All holders of the 10 cents ballot or ticket, will be entitled to admission by said ticket, and the 10 cent admission fee entitles to a vote.

The New Era
Humeston, Iowa
September 19, 1888, page 5

Chase & Stoops, Groceries

The ladies composing the various divisions of the Women's Relief Corps in Iowa are at work on a new scheme to raise money for needy veterans. They make what is known as a military quilt. All vets who pay fifty cents have their names and the number of their regiment and letter of their company worked in a block, and besides, are entitled to a chance on the quilt when it is raffled off.

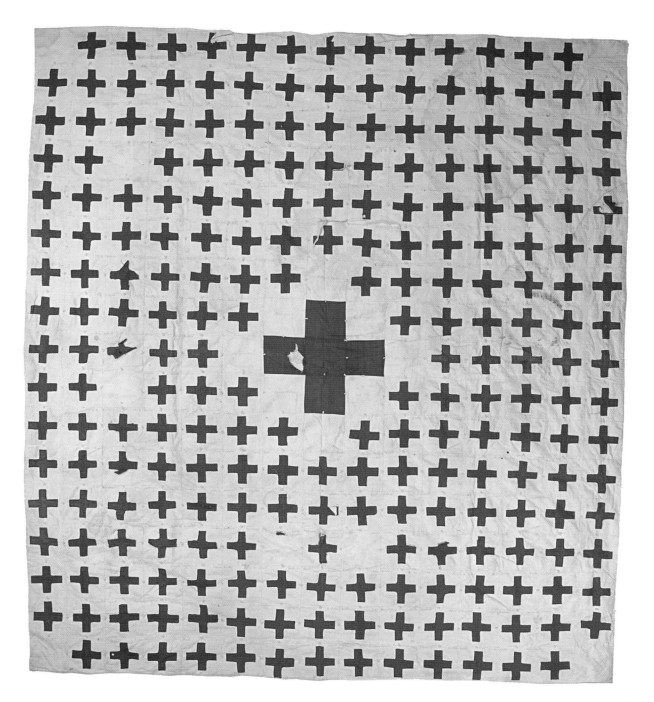

Red Cross Quilt, c. 1918, Rutland, Vermont, hand pieced, hand appliquéd, hand tied, 87 inches x 96 inches, cotton. The Red Cross quilt pattern was designed by Clara Washburn Angell of The Modern Priscilla magazine. It was published in the December 1917 issue in response to a call for increased fund raising for Red Cross and the War effort.

Iowa City Citizen
Iowa City, Iowa
December 1, 1917, page 8

ALL HONOR DUE
AGED WORKER OF RED CROSS QUILT
MADE BY AGED IOWA CITY WOMAN NETS $212
FOR RED CROSS
Patriotic Woman Helps Cause
Mrs. (Lydia) Kimball is now ninety-three years of age and is still active in the work for the country, During the past few months she has kept her needle busy and many knitted garments as well as quilts and the like have been made and the proceeds turned to the red cross, or the garment given to the relief of the soldiers. During the summer, a beautiful "goose" quilt, the work of her hands was placed on sale at Yetters' store and the proceeds turned into the Red Cross.
Not the First Time
More than a half century ago Mrs. Kimball was active in the work of the Red Cross, or "Ladies' Aid" as it was then called, and together, with many other women of the country including Mrs. Samuel Kirkwood, still living in the city and widow of Iowa's civil war governor, did much for the relief of the soldiers at the front.

Iowa Recorder
Greene, Iowa
December 12, 1917

The three Red Cross quilts, given by the Even Dozen Club, now contains 968 names, at 10 cents a name was sold for $11.00 which totals $107.80 and it was returned to be resold.

The Stevens Point Journal
Stevens Point, Wisconsin
December 22, 1917, page 6

Museum Gets Unique Quilt
Madison—A quilt containing the name and company of every member of the Brodhead, Wis., G.A.R. post was received by the G.A.R. museum in the state capital. The presentation was made by Mrs. Sarah S. Brodhead.

Iowa Recorder
Greene, Iowa
December 26, 1917

The quilt made by the Linger Longer Club on which numbers were sold was drawn by Mrs. Geo. Berkley of Allison and netted the club $13, which will be turned into some charitable fund.

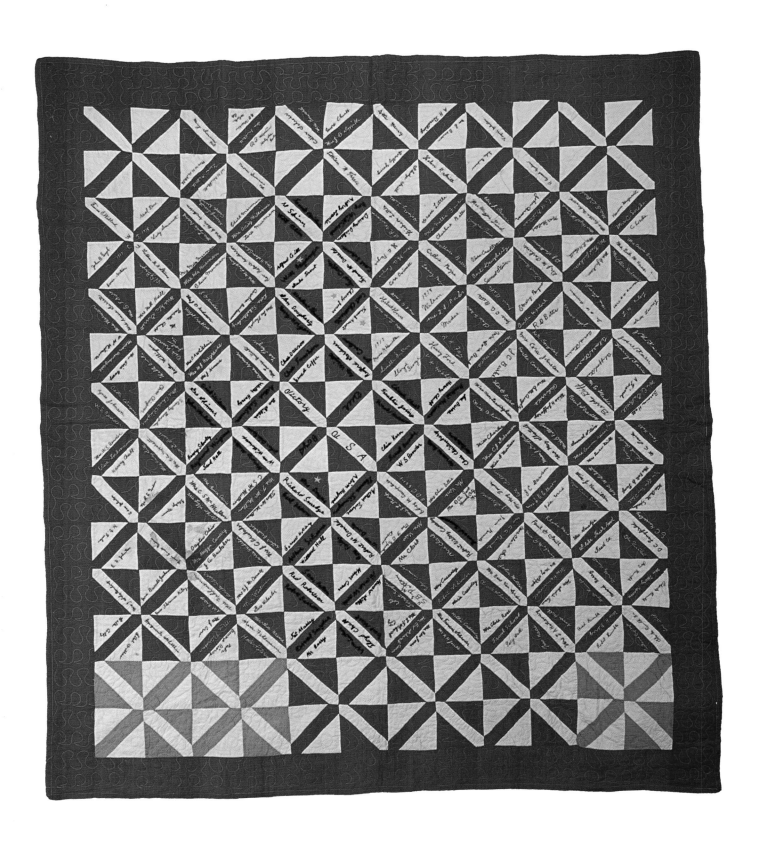

World War I Quilt, dated 1917-1918, Denver, Colorado, machine pieced, hand embroidered, machine quilted, 74 inches X 84 inches, cotton. There are approximately 400 names inscribed on this patriotic quilt from "The Great War." Gold Stars are next to the names of men who were killed in World War I. In one section of the quilt are blocks signed Carrie Nation and Frances E. Willard, important names in the WCTU. Herbert Hoover is also inscribed on the quilt but it is not known if he was our future President.

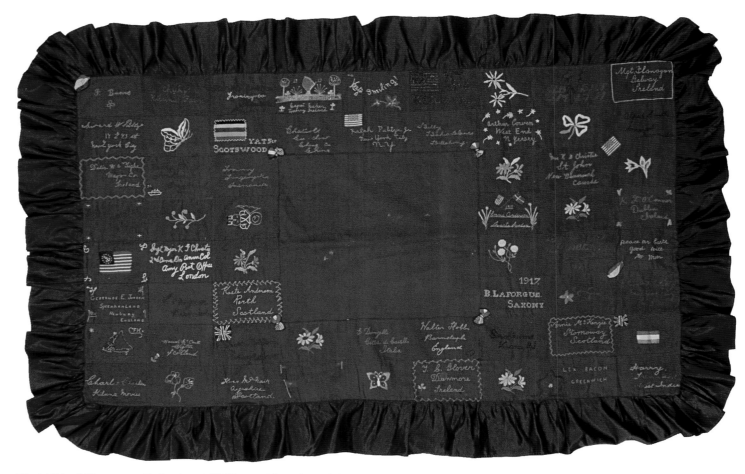

World War I Signature Quilt, dated 1917, machine pieced, hand embroidered, embellished, 66 inches x 40 inches, polished cotton. This decorative, World War I quilt has names from the United States, England, Ireland, Canada, Italy, the West Indies, Sweden, Bermuda, France, Tasmania, and Scotland.

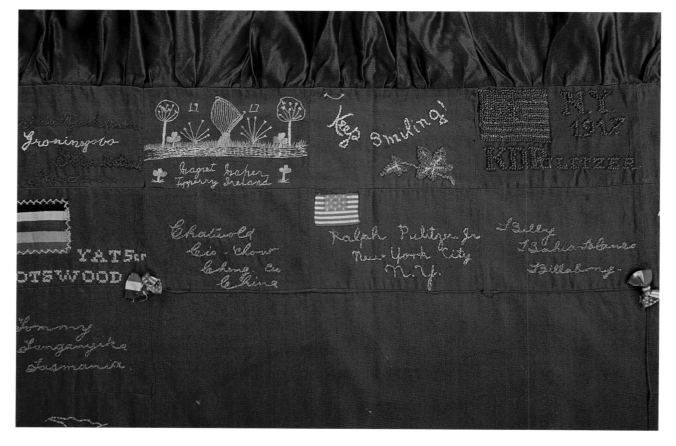

Fan Signature Quilt, Hamilton County, Indiana, c. 1920, machine pieced, hand embroidered, 82 inches x 68 inches, cotton. This quilt was most likely made to raise funds for a benevolent cause in Hamilton County, Indiana just north of Indianapolis. In addition to the names of both businesses and ministers, a Grandma and residents of Canada have their names inscribed on the quilt.

Post-WWII Chimney Sweep Signature Quilt. Hand and machine pieced, hand embroidered, hand quilted, 76 inches x 86.5 inches, cotton. This quilt possibly was made for a reunion of WWII or Korean War soldiers. The sashing is red, white and blue striped fabric.

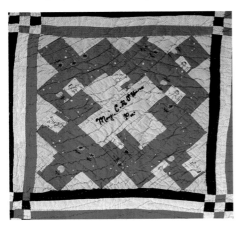

CHAPTER 5

"There must be no Idlers in Zion"

QUILTMAKING AND THE CHURCH

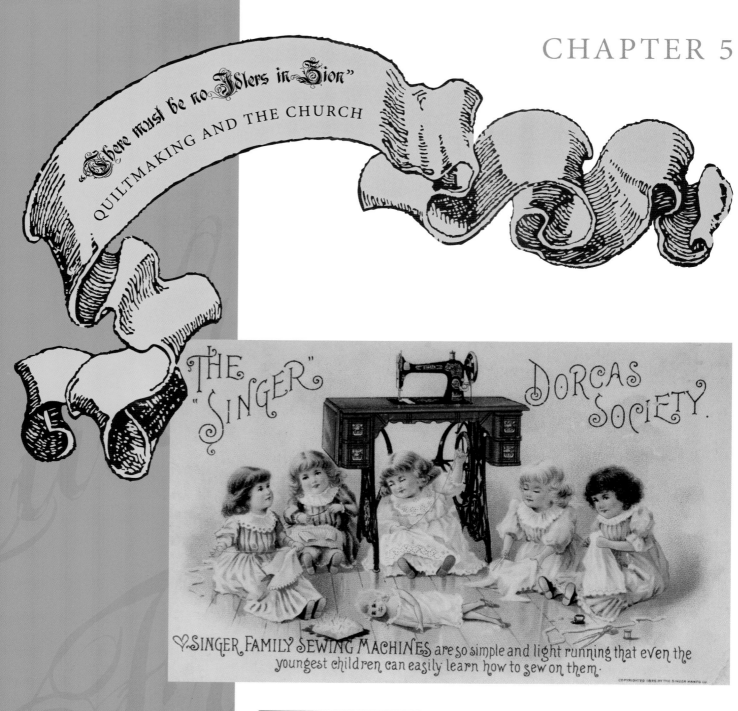

THE "SINGER" DORCAS SOCIETY.

♡ SINGER FAMILY SEWING MACHINES are so simple and light running that even the youngest children can easily learn how to sew on them.

COPYRIGHTED 1895 BY THE SINGER MANFG CO.

"Lititz, Pennsylvania. The Moravian sewing circle quilts for anyone at one cent a yard of thread and donates the money to the church." LC-USW3- 011850-D, Library of Congress Prints and Photographs Division Washington, D.C.

That's a great idea

The Davenport Daily Gazette
Davenport, Iowa
August 19, 1857, page 3

Revelations of the Miseries and Mysteries of Mormonism

From a recently issued volume on Mormonism by JOHN HYDE, formerly a Mormon elder and resident of Salt Lake City, we quote:

THE WORKING ROOM

We are then conducted to a noisy part of the house. Here, in a busy work room, is a bevy of industrious ladies—some at looms, some at spinning wheels, some at quilting frames; and high above the clatter of battens, shuttles and wheels, rises the sound of women's voices. They hush into silence on seeing brother Brigham, who then tells us how many pounds of wool they have spun, knitted and wove; the yards of linsey, flannel and carpeting they have made. Stockings and quilts are at quite a premium in this manufactory. Brigham makes all his ladies work. They have to be examples to all women of Utah; and Young's hobby cry is, "There must be no idlers in Zion."

Athens Messenger
Athens, Ohio
January 13, 1876

The ladies of the M. E. Church, of McArthur, have presented a quilt, consisting of as many kinds of calico as possible, put together with white squares, to be kept for exhibition in 1976. It will, of course, be exhibited at different times before that. They want one thousand names on it. They have now about two hundred. All persons wishing to have their names on it, can send them to Mrs. Maria Rankin, or hand them to any of the members, always accompanied with ten cents. The dime will help support the church. – *Vinton Record*

Athens Messenger
Athens, Ohio
September 14, 1876

A very pleasant affair came off at Temperance Hall last week, in the way of an old-fashioned "quilting." The ladies of Mt. Pleasant Methodist Church presented the wife of their esteemed pastor, Rev. P. Orr, a beautiful quilt.

Chester Daily Times
Chester, Pennsylvania
February 26, 1878 page 3

A NOVEL QUILT—The Ladies' Aid Soociety, connected with the Trinity M.E. Church, are superintending the making of a bed quilt, which, in its construction, is somewhat novel. The quilt will be composed of one hundred blocks, and on each block will be written in indelible ink five names; and for the privilege of having your name on one ten cents is charged; so that when it is completed it will have netted $50.

Each block is to be composed of alternate red and white patches; and upon the white patches, of which each block contains five, the names will be written, generally, in family groups, and each group is expected to make its own block. When the quilt is completed it will be presented to the Rev. Mr. Kurtz as a memorial of his flock. The proceeds will be added to the amount the above society already have, and devoted to the purchase of cushions and carpets for the church. The quilt will be very handsome when finished, and doubtless will be highly treasured by its recipient.

Oshkosh Daily Northwestern
Oshkosh, Wisconsin
April 7, 1879

The little girls of the Trinity Parish Sabbath School have completed a quilt, for some worthy poor family.

Chester Daily Times
Chester, Pennsylvania
December 8, 1880, page 1

The Autograph Bed Quilt

It was not because there was any danger that their beloved pastor, the Rev. C.W. Cooper, would suffer from cold while in bed during the approaching long winter nights that the ladies of the South Centreville Presbyterian Church resolved to present him with a bed quilt. Far from it. But they had fitted him out with almost everything else, both useful and ornamental, and as a neighboring flock had given its shepherd a sofa pillow larger by several squares of silk than ones the South Centerville ladies had a short time before surprised their pastor with, another demonstration on their part was necessary, and so the bed quilt was decided upon. It was to be an autograph quilt. Every old, young, married, and unmarried woman of the congregation was to donate a fragment of some wearing material from which the quilt was to be made. Then the autographs of all such donors or anybody else who chose to contribute the small sum of one dime was to be skillfully wrought on the patches in many-colored silk, by the needles of the fairest of the flock. Work was begun on this wonderful quilt two months ago. Long before it was finished the question of who should have the honor of presenting it to the pastor was the leading one for discussion at the meetings of the ladies. When the quilt was completed, week before last, the question was still undecided. Two prominent young ladies were rivals for the honor. Finally, to the matter without creating unsisterly feeling and making the quilt a stumbling block, it was concluded to decide by the lot who should place the quilt in the pastor's hand. The plan was to hold a social, at which the drawing was to take place. Chances were to be sold at ten cents each, the proceeds to go to the church fund. Whoever should draw a ticket inscribed, "Quilt" secured control of the privilege of presenting it.

The social was held a few nights since at the house of Brother William Davy. Everybody was there. The quilt was, gorgeous in coloring and remarkable as to autographic inscription, was prominently displayed.

There was great excitement over the taking of chances. The two young ladies were supported by their respective friends, and almost every chance sold was placed in the name of one or another of them.

Old Uncle Tunis Wood, who lives near Centreville, was passing Brother Davy's house about nine o'clock on the night of the sociable. He heard the sounds of merriment within. He knew it was a public gathering, and the purpose of it. He went in.

Uncle Tunis was surrounded by the young ladies and their friends at once. Each besought him to buy a chance for her.

"Can't choose betwixt ye," said he. I'll split the difference and buy a chance for myself." He bought one. Seven hundred and sixty chances were all that could be sold. Then the drawing commenced. After about four hundred tickets had been drawn and the prize ticket was still in the hat, Tunis Wood's name was called. He drew out a ticket. It was marked "Quilt." The old man had drawn the prize. He was besieged by each young lady to let her be his substitute in presenting the quilt to the preacher.

"The preacher! Give this quilt to the Preacher! Well, not this year, I guess. Ain't this quilt good enough for me? I guess no preacher don't git this quilt. I won it, I reckon!"

And the old man took the quilt and went home with it. A committee followed him to tell him that he didn't seem to understand the object of the drawing. He said that he thought he understood it very well. Since then the ladies have visited him and offered to make him a quilt exactly like the one he drew if he would let them have that one.

"This un suits me to death," he replied "an' I'm afeered you couldn't git them colors jist like that agin. I wouldn't like to part with it, ladies."

And at last accounts neither pleadings nor threats had induced him to change his mind. Meantime the neighboring flock remains several squares in a silk sofa cushion ahead of the South Centreville ladies, and, it is said, has a dressing gown for its shepherd nearly completed.—N.Y. Sun.

A Corner of Tent City, Ocean Grove, N. J.

The Tabernacle and Church, Oak Bluffs, Mass.

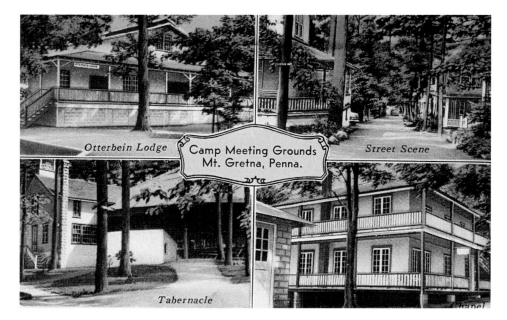

Otterbein Lodge

Camp Meeting Grounds Mt. Gretna, Penna.

Street Scene

Tabernacle

Bow Tie Methodist Episcopal Signature Quilt, c. 1890, hand and machine pieced, hand embroidered, machine quilted, 75 inches x 86 inches, cotton. This quilt is embroidered with charming images reflecting imagination and humor. The figures often poke fun at the inscribed names. The people represented on this quilt cannot be traced to a specific geographic area. This characteristic is commonly found on Church quilts (especially made by the Methodist Episcopal Church) from the last quarter of the Nineteenth Century and the early Twentieth Century. Most likely these quilts were made at the summer camp meetings held at various sites such as Oak Bluffs, Massachusetts; Ocean Grove, New Jersey; Mt. Gretna, Pennsylvania.

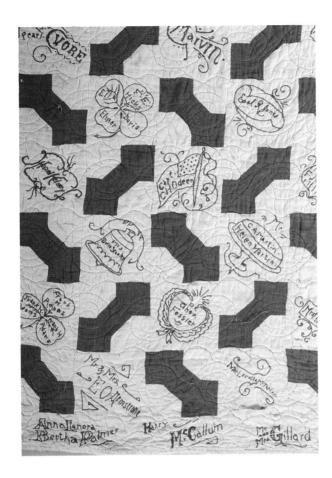

The Fresno Republican
Fresno, California
August 11, 1883, page 1

Senator Crane of Marion, Kan., offered the Ladies' Aid Society, $5 if they would make a quilt without speaking a word. Twenty-three ladies met at the parsonage, made the quilt and earned the money in two hours.

Herald & Torch Light
Hagerstown, Maryland
January 3, 1884, page 3

Fared Sumptuously

The supper and "sociable" given by the Ladies' Union of the Methodist Episcopal church last Friday night, at Mr. and Mrs. Samuel Ulrich's residence on Franklin street, was a gratifying success in every respect. One hundred and seven persons took supper during the evening, and for several hours the large dining room was a scene of clatter and bustle that would have made a hungry man's soul ache with desire. The menu embraced the best the market afforded, and it was served by the most charming attendants. The pretty waiters were young ladies all dressed alike, with brand new calico dresses, "mutton leg" sleeves, white aprons, hair done up with old-fashioned combs, on the top of the head, and the most bewitching frizzes fringing their foreheads, presenting a picture of loveliness so ravishing that it must have melted the soul of any anchorite, if one had been present. We cannot say as much for the generosity of at least one of the carvers who served the writer of this item with the two extremes of a badly used up turkey. It served, however, to illustrate how easily we can make both ends meet when we have a prudent manager at the bow and stern of the vessel. We shall get even with that carver, by and by. After the supper, quite a number remained for several hours and spent the time in pleasant social intercourse. The receipts of the evening enterprise were about $50 leaving a net profits of at least $49.50. This goes into the fund furnishing the new church.

During the evening a pleasant surprise was given Miss Nettie Baker. It was in the presentation of a beautiful album quilt containing names of those who contributed toward making it, written on different squares or patches. The quilt had been made by the ladies of the society during several years past, and the finishing touches were put upon it only the morning of the day. The presentation was made by Capt. Seidenstricker, in a neat little speech, and responded to (for Miss Baker) by Mr. Seybold. It was a genuine surprise to Miss Baker, and a very pleasant winding up of an evening of real enjoyment. The ladies feel very grateful to all who encouraged them in this enterprise, and through this medium express many sincere thanks, with a cordial invitation to come again, next time.

Marion Daily Star
Marion, Ohio
July 18, 1885, page 4

—Next Wednesday evening, July 22nd, the ladies of the German Evangelical Prot. Church will give an ice cream and raspberry festival at Music Hall. At the same time they will sell a quilt for which they sell tickets at twenty-five cents each, and can be had at H. Ackerman's music store. The receipts will for the benefit of their new church on east South street. Admission free.

West Nashville Aux. and Watertown U.S. Presbyterian Auxiliary Quilt, dated 1932, machine pieced, hand embroidered, hand quilted, 66.5 inches x 99 inches, cotton. Approximately 600 names from the Nashville area were embroidered on this quilt. The event or occasion for the creation of the quilt has not been determined.

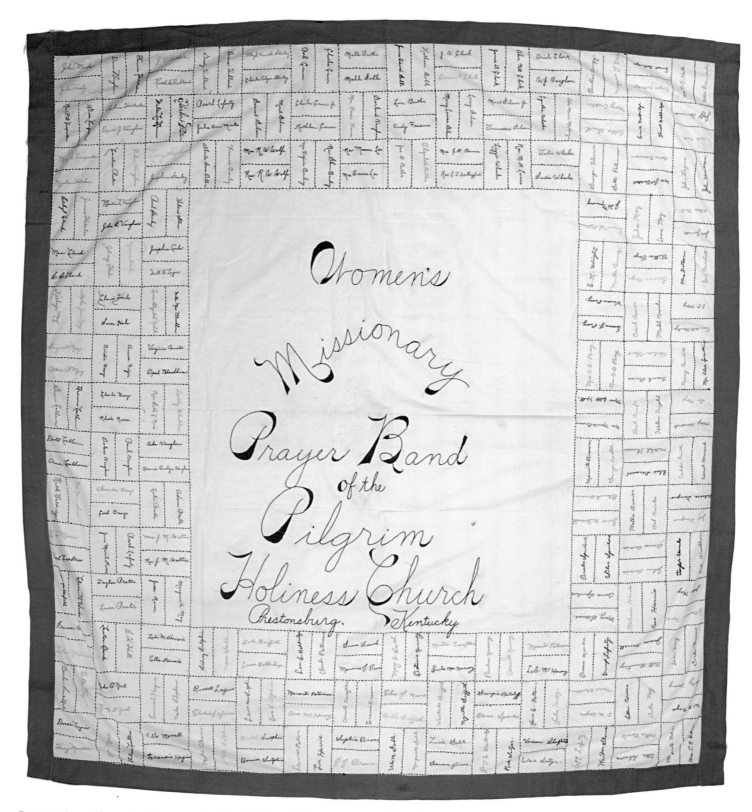

Prestonsburg, Kentucky Signature Quilt, c. 1930, machine constructed, hand embroidered, 76 inches x 82.5 inches, cotton. Prestonsburg, at the foothills of the Appalachian Mountains in Floyd County, is known as "The Star City of Eastern Kentucky."

Wide-Awake Circle Basket Quilt Top, dated 1933, Grand Rapids, Michigan, machine pieced, machine appliquéd, hand embroidered, 68 inches x 82 inches, cotton.

Charleroi Mail
Charleroi Mail
Charleroi, Pennsylvania
March 1, 1934, page 3

An entertaining and charming social affair of yesterday afternoon was a "Patchwork Party" given by a group of women of the Ladies' Aid Society of the Methodist Episcopal church in the church parlor. Approximately fifty members and guests were served luncheon at 1 o'clock following which the remaining hours up till four o'clock were spent in cutting and sewing quilt patches.

So Sweet !
Look this
task !

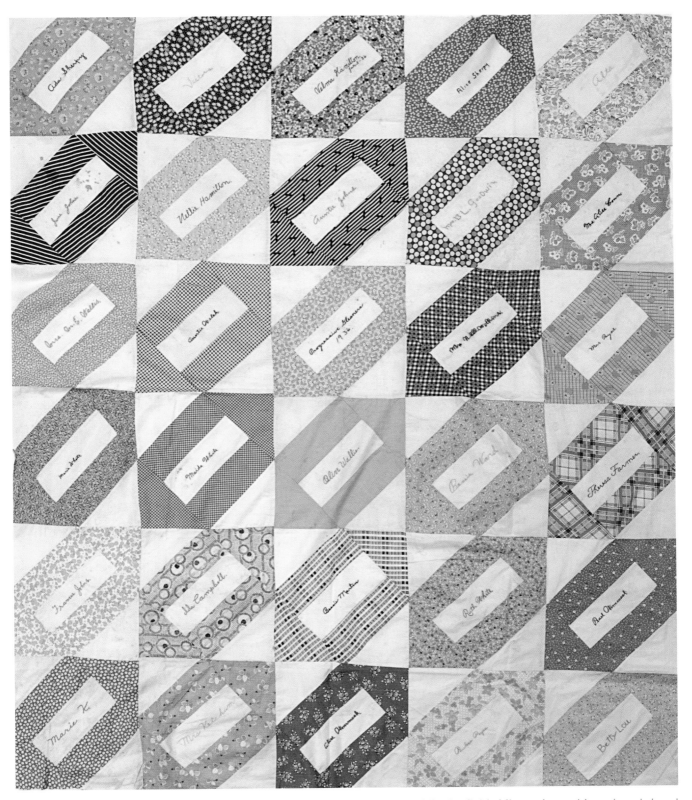

Progressive Gleaners Chain Link Quilt, dated 1936, North Campbell and Springfield, Missouri, machine pieced, hand embroidered, 65 inches x 76 inches, cotton.

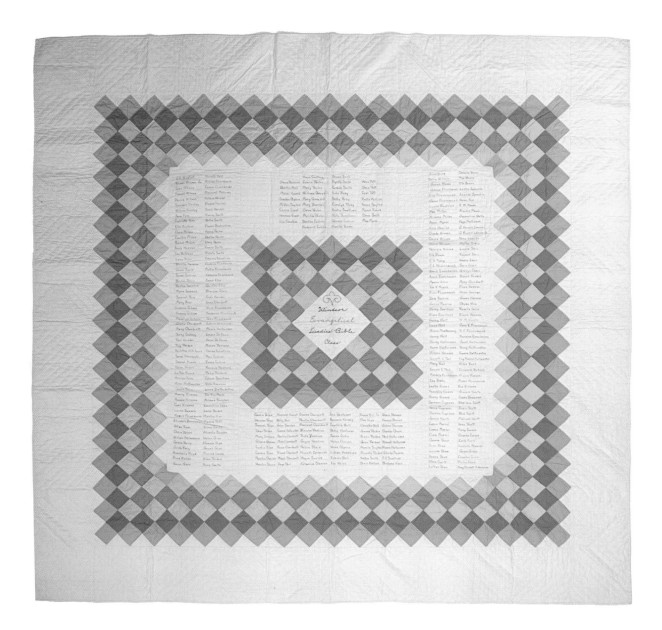

Windsor Evangelical Church Quilt, c. 1935, Windsor, York, Pennsylvania, machine pieced, hand quilted, hand embroidered, inked names, hand appliqué, cotton. This quilt was pieced in the very popular quilt pattern, Philadelphia Pavement design. It was very precisely signed in a neat, easy-to-read script. Collection of Barbara Garrett

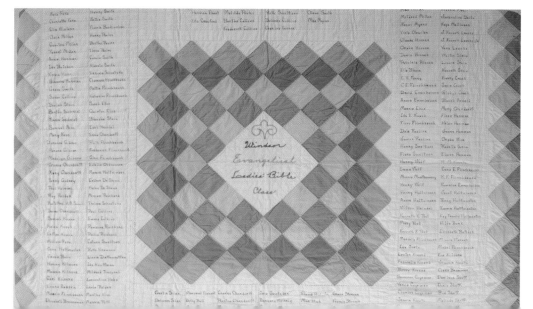

ROW 2: Martha Downs, Cora A. Crittendon, David Hill, Edward S. Rodgers, Mrs. W.H. Davenport, Geo. S. Hurd, Edward D. Whitney, Arthur T. Hunt

ROW 3: Jennie Stewart, Bert T. Whitney, Fred P. Whitney, Fannie M. Gillmore, Mrs. John Sener???, W.W. Wilde, Rena M. Hurd, Henry F. Webb

ROW 4: Chas Hull, Ralph J. Langdon, Charles Spring, Mary S. Smith, S.T. Hurd, S.V. Halsey, William H. Nye, George S. Bosworth

ROW 5: Mrs. T.J. Owen, Arthur Waters, Mrs.F.M. Bliss, Elson J. Kinne, Elmore J. Kinne, Harvey Tillotson, Sherwood J. Rogers, Mrs. Elmore Bills

ROW : B.H. Tainter, Frank M. Bliss, Fred W. Kimberley, Miss Julia E. Ward, Rev. W.A. Fobes, Amanda J. Whitney, George W. Stewart, Ellsworth J. Kenne

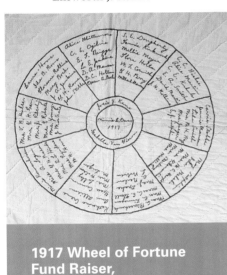

1917 Wheel of Fortune Fund Raiser, Brooklyn, New York

CENTER: Josie Y. Kane, Minnie L. Owens, Isabella Van Gieson

SPOKE 1: Alice Whittemore, C.E. Ogivie, E.F. Briggs, L.E. Jenkins, D.A. Manson, D.C. Holton, Oscar A. Buch

SPOKE 2: S. E. Dougherty, Fannie Kirkwood, Mellie Meyers, Flora Holton, W.F. Corinth, G. H. Perry, Millard Manden

SPOKE 3: C. C. Bisbee, Alice Martin, C. E. Kuhnle, E. A. Smith, David Martin, J. H. Rollins

SPOKE 4: Carrie Stabbe, Jennie Manson, Lida Smith, Mrs. W. H. Way, Mrs. Jaeger, E. J. Sutphim

SPOKE 5: May Sutphin, Ida Welsh, Mrs. W. C.Haupt, Mrs. Gilmartin, Mrs. Sterling, Mrs. Mallisen

SPOKE 6: Mrs. C. Bierschenk, Mrs. E. Finnegan, Mrs. C. E. Gisell, Mrs. J. Drake, c. Barlow, L. Wolven

Katherine Crane, Ann Allison, Grace Cameron, Mrs. Lobley, Mrs. Watson, M. Lugar

Minne Koumenhoven, Miss A. Logan, Mrs. G. H. Nason, Mrs. R. L. Hinds, Mrs. Rynders, W. H. Horne

Mrs. V. B. Hulse, Mrs. G. H. Frew, Mrs. J. Ritschy, Mrs. G. Roberts, Mrs. Young, J. MacCrate

Laura Howe, Ida B. Rowe, Florence Rollins, Mary Boch, J. A. Jenkins, G. H. Rowe, John Stabbe

1917 – 1918 World War I Quilt, Denver, Colorado

ROW 1:

Block 1 – Catherine Bigcraft, Charles Rumble Sr., Eva Liff

Block 2 – Robert Rumble, Mrs. H Berry, Fred Rumble

Block 3 – Theo Haas, Mrs. L.A. Hathaway, Anna Hall

Block 4 – Mrs. Clara Rosa, Frank Schwab, Lucy Wall

Block 5 - Nellie Cassidy, Mrs. Frances Schroder, Mr. R H James

Block 6 – Mrs. Rose James, Mr. Ed Schwab (Canon), Mrs. L. F. Schwab (City)

Block 7 – Wm Luther, Floyd Chubb, Earl Mark

Block 8 – Fat Massey, Orval Snyder, Mr Berry

Block 9 – Martha Harris, Maria Fehlmann, Helen Peterson

Block 10 - ??? Emma Pierce, Mrs. Peterson, Mrs. J Crow

Block 11 – Marguerite Schulthers???

Block 12 – Ethel Gillis, Della Colby

ROW 2:

Block 1 – Charles Rumble, Mrs. Mary Hansen, Mary Rumble

Block 2 – Myrtle Rumble, Howard Berry, Dorothy Rumble

Block 3 – Mrs. Sadie Turner, Mrs. Hammond, Mrs. Mary Stippe

Block 4 – John Miller, Mrs. Becc Van ???, Claude Shattuck

Block 5 - May Cassidy, Robert Schroder, Marie Cassidy

Block 6 – Forrest Snyder (Colo), (U S M) S B Patton, Edw Cassidy

Block 7 - Howard Gibbs, Monroe Woods, Minor Coon

Block 8 – Sam Patton, Red Patton, Robert Patto

Block 9 - Mrs. E. J. McDonnell, Mrs. Westman, Gus Wheeler

Block 10 – A M Berry, Mrs. Fehlmann, Blanche Schroer

Block 11 – Mrs. Burrell Jackson, Mrs. Florence Riley

Block 12 – Mrs. J Schellenberg

ROW 3:

Block 1 - Lela Van Fleet, D C Langfield, E C Hensley

Block 2 – Mrs. Smabye, Globe Fuel and Feed Co.

Block 3 – Rhoda Ward, Paul G Smith, Mrs. G. W. Young

Block 4 – Mrs. Clara Smith, Mrs AA Parmalee, Irene Purnell

Block 5 – Mrs. Clark, Robert Victory Cassidy, Leonard Timmons

Block 6 – Mr. Clark, Mrs Vine, Mrs F B Spratlin (Denver)

Block 7 – Roy Reily, Robert McDonald, Wm Davis

Block 8 – Earnest Holday, Arthur Schoene, Willard Hall

Block 9 – Carrie Brubaker, Mrs J C Brubaker, Arthur Brubaker

Block 10 – Dayton Ohio, Mrs Maggie Canary, J A Brubaker

Block 11 – Morris Everett Gordan

Block 12 – E.H. Johnston, H. G. Fisher

ROW 4:

Block 1 – Miss Ruth Speaker, Mrs. Lora Van Fleet, Mrs. Kate E Lang

Block 2 – Miss Anna Dolan, Miss J Hamilton, Robert W Schott

Block 3 – J C Dawson, Mrs E Ellison, Ida Ward

Block 4 – E J Greene, Mrs Mary Bender, Rose Gillem

Block 5 – Mrs. Olive Ellie, Mr Vine, Mr O A Jack (Kansas City)

Block 6 – Mrs J L Thorp, Obray M Campbell, BDC 441-1

Block 7 – Arthur Tichner, Thomas Flanagan, Alvin Haynes

Block 8 – Gold Star Geo Bouger, Richard Smebye, Earl Brown

Block 9 – Thos McMullen, Mrs. T McMullen, C S McMullen

Block 10 – Mrs. Anna Davis, Mrs CS McMullen, Mrs Lizzie Shillito

Block 11 – Gladys Meuer, Mr. R E Gordon

Block 12 – Edna Johnston

ROW 5:

Block 1 – (Iowa) Claude Chubb, W G Smith, Fern Hall

Block 2 – Samuel Stein, Mrs. Emma Reeder (PA), Mrs Laura Neill

Block 3 – Miss J Griffith, Mrs May Shattuck, Miss E Pellenz

Block 4 – Miss Charles, Mrs C J Godsman, Miss G Montrose

Block 5 – Norman Betts, Chas Christianbury, Geo Patterson

Block 6 – Claire Kern, Frank Bender, W S Bender

Block 7 – USA

Block 8 – Boys

Block 9 – Harry Muller, Wm Witherwax, John Dickson

Block 10 – Henry Scholtz, Raymond Weigand , Fred Hall

Block 11 – Mrs. Daisy Gill, Mrs. E A Happersett, Eva G. Grace

Block 12 – Mrs. W.S. Bender, Elsie Lochmans, Harvey Chubb

ROW 6:

Block 1 – Bernice Hall, Mr E Galbreth, A Friend

Block 2 – M E Madden, Bertha Diff, Paul Stardley

Block 3 – Miss H Jafferay, Valverde, Mrs Ella Wayle

Block 4 – Mibbs G Ridel, Miss Van Landingham, Miss Bliss

Block 5 – Jas Burns, Herbery Mermon, Harvey Chubb

Block 6 – Claude Chubb, Franklin Jaring, Harold Anderson

Block 7 – Our

Block 8 – Victory

Block 9 – Leo Gillies, Arthur Fehlman, Walter Henry

Block 10 – Dick Wilson, Geo Skinner, John Waldow

Block 11 – Stanley Livingston, Mrs. Chas Clingner, Chas. Clingner

Block 12 – Della Clingner, Agnes Johnson, W S Bende

ROW 7:

Block 1 – J W Karn, Jos??? Karn, Harry Karn

Block 2 – Clifford Karn, Clare Karn, Doris Karn

Block 3 – Kate Snyder, Mrs Cora Johnston, Bertha Conrad

Block 4 – J C Burke, Marie Simmons, Mrs Dora Burke

Block 5 – R F Fay, Henry Ford, V K Hoehl

Block 6 – 1917 Maria N. Hamilton, Lucella Sutton, Lloyd George

Block 7 – Roy Wright, Redford Gardener, Joe Carlson

Block 8 – Chas Dawson, Chas Tuncheon, Ernest Coffer

Block 9 – Irma Armour, Mrs Laura Boutswell, Leo Thayer

Block 10 – Mrs D A Whitehair, Mrs M J Hargraves, Mrs J Armour

Block 11 – Mable Burke, Bertha Milligan, Osie Needels Joplin Mo.

Block 12 – Mrs. Doris Penny, Marion Prendergrast, WW Wilmore

ROW 8:

Block 1 – Mrs. G W Anman, L W Riley, Sam Lunng???

Block 2 – John Armour, Dr O W Au???, Mrs Leung

Block 3 – Emery Payne, Arthur McIntosh, R D Betts

Block 4 – Chas A Betts, Mrs C A Betts, Irene Betts

Block 5 – 1918 Wilson, Mrs J S Baker, Midar

Block 6 – Mrs Laura Wells, Herbert Hoover, Mrs L C Smith

Block 7 – Gold Star Frank Arndt, Carl Chatrelle, Gold Star Chancy Jones

Block 8 – Herbert Thomas, Glen Dougherty, Harry Morgan

Block 9 – Mrs Leo Thayer, Dora Schellenberg, Caroline Buckmann

Block 10 – J O Anderson, Mrs. J O Anderson, Hazel Crabtree

Block 11 – Mo. Lucille Chubb, Mrs. Ida Garrett, Mrs Ida Garrett

Block 12 – Lois Merman, Mrs. Anna Garrett, Mrs E T Guire

ROW 9:

Block 1 – Mrs. Anna Brown, Mrs. Leah M Haas, Mrs. Ella Redman

Block 2 – Mrs. E. Jackson, Mr. Fred Jackson, Mrs. L.H. Smith

Block 3 – Frank Bender, Dr. J. W. Perkins, D. J. Sullivan

Block 4 – Vera Crabtree, Bert Daugherty, Samuel Stein

Block 5 – Wallace Betts Arthur Payne, Lacey Payne

Blocks 6 – Cora Duinell, Mrs. H A Payne, H A Payne

Block 7 – Fred Coffer, Frank McDonald, Carl Schoen

Block 8 – Alfred Gill, Gold Star Will Baysinger, Luke Trout

Block 9 – Mrs M Loughery, Rev Robert Anderson, Mrs Helen Eliot

Block 10 – Mrs. Meta Merman, Mrs Ida Housman, Clare Merman

Block 11 – W. J. Bryan, Lillian M. N. Stevens

Block 12 – John B Gough, Carrie Nation 1917 WCTU 1918

ROW 10:

Block 1 – Herman Marguadt, Mrs. C. Losche, C. Losche

Block 2 – Mrs. Hazel McComb, Mrs. Bertha Underwood, Mrs. E. Dillard

Block 3 – Mrs. Miller, G. W. Gillies, John Brower

Block 4 – Mrs. J. Brown, Mrs. Maggie Lind, Engra Lind

Block 5 – Grace Little, Mrs. Nellie Fouler, Charlie Betts

Block 6 – S R Weigand, Hickson Little, Dorothy Little

Block 7 – Dewey Dickson, Roy Williams, Aubrey Loomis

Block 8 – Frank Ogilire, M Skinner, Will Olin

Block 9 – Edith Merman, Mrs. Daisy Williams, Lois Merman

Block 10 – Mrs. Lydia Paddock, Mrs. Elsie Anderson, Irving Smith, Camp Kearney

Block 11 – Neal Dow., Lady Sommerset

Block 12 – Frances E Willard

ROW 11:

Block 3 – R. Ernest Gordan

Block 4 – Ida Gradman

Block 5 – Helen R Smith

Block 6 – Gladys Smith, Dorothy Young

Block 7 – Lillian M Throw?

Block 8 – Naomi Summer, Neb.

Block 9 – W H Hubbell, Leona Hubbell, Mrs. W H Hubbel

ROW 12:

Block 4 – Virginia Johnston

Block 5 – Mrs. E Benson, A H Findling

Block 6 – Dollie Meway???

Block 7 – Laura Chubb, Mrs. J E Smith

Block 8 – Arthur Schroder, Mrs. Howard

Block 9 – R T Martin, Holyoke, Colo., Ida Hubbell, B Martin, Holyoke, Colo; Mary Summers, Neb.

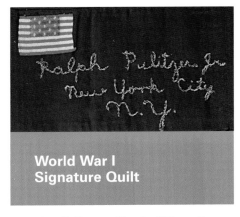

World War I Signature Quilt

ROW 1: G. Burns; Cheeky Kiluna Farms; Mathilda Bjarhegreen Groningsba – Blanka? Sweden; Magret Maher – Tipperary, Ireland; Keep Smiling; K D Blitzer, N.Y. 1917; Albert Smith; Mgt. Flanagan – Galway, Ireland

ROW 2: ??? W ???; Butterfly; Yats Scotswood; Chatwold Cia-chow Cheng, Cu Chine; Ralph Pulitzer Jr – New York, N.Y.; L Silly – Bahia-Blanca, Billabong; Arthur Cowan – West End, N Jersey; Alfred Smith – Somerset, Bermuda

ROW 3: Dalia M & Tighe – Mayo, Co. Ireland; Ella Prow – Southsea, England; Sonny – Langanyiks, Tasmania; Mrs K A Christie – St Johns, New Brunswick, Canada

ROW 4: Fred J. Knotts, Niedfluh; 1917 - Emma Anderson, Ivarte Sweden; K.F. O'Connor, Dublin, Ireland

ROW 5: Sgt Mjor K G Christie – 2nd ???, Army Post Office, London; Peace on Earth Good Will to Men

ROW 6: Gertrude E. Jordon. Speenhamland. Newbury. England: L. Fagan – Bermuda; Kate Anderson – Perth, Scotland; 1917 - B. Laforelle – Saxony; Elizabeth Tully – New York City U.S.A.

ROW 7: Sailboat – FH; Hannah McCaull, Wigton, Scotland; F.M. Wilson, England; E. Danzelli, Citta di Castella, Italia; Walter Hobbs – Barnstable, England; Snockums – Verona, N.J.; Annie McKenzie, Stornoway, Scotland

ROW 8: Charlie Chaplin – Kiluna Movies; Flora McNair – Ayershire, Scotland; Mary Warren – Kilcormac, Knigs Co, Ireland, Y. C. Glover – Dunmore, Ireland; Lex Bacon – Greenwich; Harry Trinidad, West Indies.

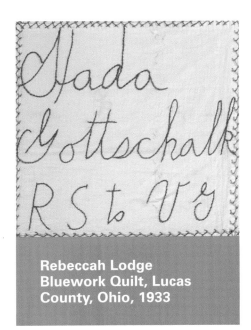

Rebeccah Lodge Bluework Quilt, Lucas County, Ohio, 1933

ROW 1: Gertie Bisher – Piano, Ella B. Harmon – Rec Sec, Edna Biglin – Fin. Sec, Jennie Burton – Tres, Babe Hulie – Tres.

ROW 2: Emma Drager – Warden; Laura Grasser – Int. Co; Elizabeth Bueher – N. G., Lida Hover – r. S. to N. G., Nina Welmer – Con. Martha Myers – Int. Co., Lena Moor – P. G., Lucas Rebeccah Lodge, Elizabeth Dutridge – Chap, May Langshore – Sick Co
Cora Kalmbach – Int Co., Florence Karon – In. G., Bertha Klukie – Aut. G., Jennie Burten – Sick Co.
Laura Grasser – Int. Co., Mamie Ditman – L. S. to V. G., Hada Gottschalk – R. S. to V. G., Gertie Bisher – Sick Co.
Lida Hover – Trus., Gertie Taylor – Fin. Co., Nora Hills – Fin. Co., Mary Grushaler – Fin. Co., Slada Gottschalk – Trus.

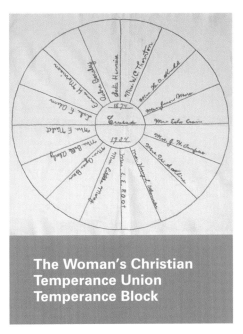

The Woman's Christian Temperance Union Temperance Block

Mrs. W. C. Thornton, Mrs. K. O. Kuhl, Mrs. Jason More, Mrs. E? Cain, Mrs. J. H. Tempar, Mrs. W. S. Kline, Mrs. Henry L. Odamster, Mrs. E. E. Root, Mrs. Estelle Morey, Mrs. Agnes Bean, Mrs. Belle Akerly, Mrs. F. Nisbet, Lulu F. Adams, Emma H. Morrison, Aubra Beasley, Sadie Henneise, Mrs. W. C. Thornton

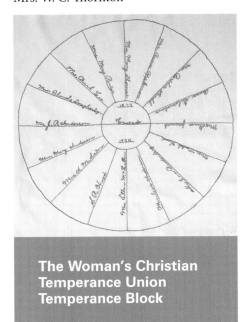

The Woman's Christian Temperance Union Temperance Block

Mr. J.R. Anderson, Mrs. Mary Anderson, Mrs. A Easton, S.A. Wood, Mrs. Ellen McCallen, Mrs. Eva Anderson, Mrs. Cora Bradenberg, Mrs. Mabel Wood, Mrs. Grace Yearick, Anna Gildersleeve, Mrs. Bertha Kuhl, Mrs. Anna Appleman, Mrs. Mary Thomas, Mrs. Mary Peters, Mrs. Pearl Lee, Mrs. Blanche Dougherty

Post WWII Chimney Sweep Signature Quilt

ROW 1: CWO H. J. Benn, Calif.; M/Sgt. C. E. Brockseiper, Calif.; Mr. L. F. Mullen, Mich.; Mr. E. J. England, Fla.; SFC. H. M. Hewitt, Pa.

ROW 2: Maj. E.W. Malloy, Texas; Maj. W. A. Evans, Okla.; Maj. C. R. O'Hara,; Maj. Toby Rizzo, N.J.; Maj. C. P. Oberbiter, Illinois

ROW 3: Maj. R. H. Lehman, Pa.; Col. R. L. Klee, Illinois; Lt. Col. J. W. Durham, Okla.; Lt. Col. R. J. Russell, West Va.; Maj. L. H. Waters, Idaho

ROW 4: Maj. J. C. Printice, N.Y.; Capt. P. R. Eckman, Ma.; Capt. John Kulik, Illinois; Capt. R. C. Allen; Capt. Joe Shevick, N.Y.

ROW 5: Lt. H. E. Wald, N. Dak.; Lt. R. E. Morton, Okla.; Lt. E. L. Wallace, Kans.; Lt. L. J. Muraro, Fla.; Capt. C. L. Viviano, Illinois

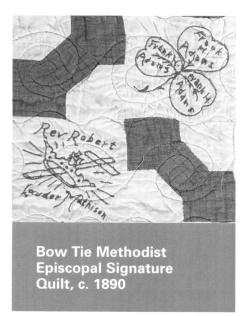

Bow Tie Methodist Episcopal Signature Quilt, c. 1890

ROW 1: Mrs. Nellie Barton – Wayne, Madeline & Mrs. C Morgan, Mrs. Russell, Margueritte McLennon, Allen & J. Richardson, Mrs. R. Springmeyer, F. J. Oldnan???, Mrs M. E. Rector

ROW 2: Mrs. Hunt, Mrs. E Lerch, Rev. E.L. Jones, Worh McClure, W Wesley, Earl R Jones, C.A. Martin, Helen Martin, Mrs. Lucetta M. Taylor

ROW 3: Mrs. Lillian Donalley, Mrs. Emily Anderson, H. F. & Annie McCallum, Wallace & Lyle, Mr. & Mrs. J.B. Kelly, Gelia, Myrnie, Homer, Hobert, Mrs. Mary Palmer, Catherine, Emma, Bertha, Mr. & Mrs. Arthur Freeburg, Marvin, Capt. C.H. Odeen, Dr. Theo Fessler

ROW 4: Mrs. A. S. Osborn, George Strum, Ray Strum, Miss Cora Brate, F. J. Steinmetz, Allie H. Steinmetz, Mrs. Hattie E. Lang, F.E. Hicks, Ella, Doris, Elmer, Mrs. Belle Stanley, Mr. & Mrs. E.O. Armstrong

ROW 5: Mrs. S. C. Crosswhite, Smith Bros., Mrs. A. E. Lacy, Miss Maria Nelan, Pearl Russell, Mrs. Vore, Eva, Pearl, Hazel Kelsey, Frank H. Adams

ROW 6: Mrs. Mary Fleck, Chas. M. Thompson, Mrs. McAllister, Wallace Carside, Mr. & Mrs. Riley Davis & Tige, Glapha Agnes Brown, Harold West, Rev. Robert Lauder Mathison

ROW 7: Mrs. W.E. Bates, Jack Daily, J.L. Smith, Mr. Tracy Johnson, Mr. Corrie Johnson, Neva Johnson, Mrs. D. Arnold, Mr. & Mrs. S.W. Simmons, Sadie & Guy, Chas E Catlow, Irene M, Lillie M., Ernest W., Winifred G., Eleanor J. Mr F.L. & Mrs. Ellen M. Peterson, Mr. C.C. Halstead, Elmer & Harry

ROW 8: Mrs. E. C. Spriggs, I. W. Spriggs, R. L. Davy, Emma Everett, Mr. & Mrs. Fleck, Beatrice, Dorothy, Mr. & Mrs. Freeburg, Mr. Ulysuss H. Mrs. Sellick, Midred E., W.E. Hoffer, Nellie C., C.B. Kicks, Bertha, Carlton, Ruth, Frederick Southard, Cedric

ROW 9: Clarence Honsberger, Mr. & Mrs. Anderson, Treasure, Otis, J. H. Reeve, Bertha E. Reeve, M. & Mrs. J. B. Springer, Mr. & Mrs. H. E. Brown, W. H. Hampton, Mrs. W. H. Hampton, Rev. & Mrs. J. W. McDougall, H E Brown, Jr, Buster Brown, Tege

ROW 10: Mrs. B. C. Stanley, Mrs. H O Canfield, J. R. lamb, Mrs. Willard Warriner, Basil, Harold, Bernice, Raymond Donahay, Mrs. W H Bickell, Genevieve, Violet Johnson, Fay, Arthur Shaffer

ROW 11: Mrs H. A. Hagalton, Rev. S. J. Kester, Mrs S. J. Kester, Roy, Mina, Mrs. F Fleck, Mrs. SJ Garside, Florence Garside, Rachel Miller, Kents, Gail Borden, Herbert, Teddie Freeman, Mrs. Halstead, Mrs. Emma Carson

ROW 12: Louise Erikson, Lizzie E. Parker, K. E. Parker, Louella Rawson, S. Mary Feighner, Floyd Geo., Mrs. J.H. Kendall, Harold Kendall, and Zella, Mrs. H. H. Osborn, Mrs. C. E. Brown, Mary Smith, Harold, William Jr., Mr. F. Lurch

ROW 13: G. N. Farrar, Mrs. Ella Jones, Cora E. Combs, Fostoria & Brubaker, Mr & Mrs. J. Benfield, Mr. Mrs. A.J. Lighty, Robert George West, Carl Francis West, John Thomas West

ROW 14: Velma, Sallie, Mr. J.D., Howard, Wallace Coleman, J. W. Reed, Mary Gregg, Ruth Gregg, Mr. F.A. Hultberg, Mrs. F.A. Hultberg, C.A. Stern

ROW 15: Mrs. Theo Fessler, J.M. McAllister, Mr. Harry Vore, Mrs. Emma Carson, H E Brown Jr, Buster Brown, Tege, Mr. Halstead, Elmer & Harry, Frank H. Adams

ROW 16: Mabel Fraser, Elzo & A Van Winkle, M. & Mrs Geo Hansell, M. F. Lurch, Fay, Arthur Shaffer, Freddrick Southard, Cedric, Rev. Robert Lauder Mathison, Mr. & Mrs. E. O. Armstrong

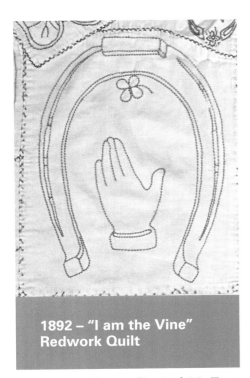

1892 – "I am the Vine" Redwork Quilt

BORDER: E.L. Harvey, "In God We Trust December 1st, 1892." M.S, Slinker, C.L. Heltman, E.L. Bennett, L. Bennett, M. J. Harvey, F. M. Berry, L. Moore, L.M. Berry, M.G./J. Englert, R. A. Heltman, "I The AM Vine." C.L. Ungard, L. V. Bitner, M.K. Leitzell, S.M. Slinker, A.L. Bitner, S.J. Englert, J.V. Leitzell

Ruffled Redwork Church Quilt, 1898 and 1899

ROW 1:

Block 1 – Mitta Good, Ethel Good, Miriam Owen, Herbert Smith, M. Kirby, Ed. Kirby, B Reeze, H.C. Chambers, H. Stewart, G. Croghan, M. Chambers, Miss Travers

Block 2 – A.L. Lyle, D.M. Campbell, D.L. Perine, T.S. Margins, D.W. Stanley, S.B. Wilson, M. Frank, M.D. Woodland, E.L. Wirt, M. R. Sake

Block 3 – Tampa, Dr. & Mrs. Oppenheimer, Hortense, Dorothy, Olive, Irma, Mr. Marcus, Mrs. Dalton, Birdie & Margie Reynolds

Block 4 – Dearest BooBoo, June 19 – 1898, K. Summerlin, Doctor, F.V. Holland, L. Marcus, L. Johnson, T. A. Torrey

Block 5 – G.H. Perine, B. F. Harn, A. Simpson, J.S. Harden, Sadie Daniels, Lucille Bagget, Dr. Wade, Helen, Major Wolff, C. Towles

Block 6 – Miss L.L. Gibbon, Mrs. R.M. Smith, A.D. Alderman

ROW 2:

Block 1 – J.S. Hollingworth. Supt., W.F. Alderman., Miss Songmire., Arthur Williams. Prin., Miss Davenport., Miss Granger., Mrs. Bailey "Miss Maud", Miss Hicks, Miss Humphries, Maude Hooker, 1898 & 99

Block 2 – S.F.M.I., Gen. E.M. Law., Col. E.M. Law, Jr., Maj. W.L. Law., Capt. T.W. Gary – Faculty. 1898 & 99, Mrs. E.M. Law, Mrs. Louise Law, Mrs. Lize Law, Latta Law, Mrs. Willie Gary, Mr. P.B. Johnston, Mrs. Annie Johnston, Mr. E.A. Law

Block 3 – H. Henry, A. Hovey, Alva, E. Hovey, Wiley. Wheeler, W. Raymond, S.C. Briton, A Raymond, Steamer Gray Eagle, J.F. Menge, Capt., M.J. P. ???, M. English

Block 4 – Robert Oglesby, Mrs. C. P. Freeman, ???, Norma Blood, Edwin Webster, Earnest Morrow

Block 5 – T.L. Marquis, M.M. Dunlope, B.B. Tatum, E. Forsyth, C. H. Wilson, C. Mather, L. F. Thurston, M. F. Tatum, V. D. Mitchell, J.T. Dunlope

Block 6 – Frances Hensell., Merger Gatlin, Karl Watson, Ethel Edwards, Mrs. Martha Hensell, Nihelia Hensell, Emmett Tore, Jasper C. Ferrell, Mrs. E. Harmon, Robert F. Hensell

ROW 3:

Block 1 – R. P. Henderson, L. D. Henderson, S,J, G, Dunlap, M. Kennedy, M. P. Kirkwood, H. F. Dietrich, O. W. Blood, B. E. Blood, B.M. Barrow, A.M. Barrow

Block 2 – Presbyterian Ladies Aid Society, H.B. Blount, Bradley, the Poet, M. Wilson, Mrs. Hollingsworth, A.E. Reed, Bertha ????, Baby Hughes, J.E. Weir, C. F. Carpenter

Block 3 – Peace on Earth, Bible, Rev & Mrs. Goldwe?, Rev. & Mrs. Brown, Rev. ?? Williamson, Pastor 1879, Pastors from 1886 to 1898

Block 4 – Faith, Pastor Waldo ??? & Wife. Rev & Mrs. Hair,???, ???

Block 5 – W.W. Willis., M.T. Dunlope., H.M. Dunlope., S.W. Ingersoll, E. A. Ingersoll, J.H. Woodard, W.E. Dunlope, H. E. Starkey

Block 6 – M. Perry, R. Lasher, Duckie White, Miss Gretta McKinley, P???, Frankie and Carrie.

ROW 4:

Block 1 – Mrs. Simons, Mrs. ???, Mrs. T. E. Wait, Mrs. J. Wilkey

Block 2 – T. Watson, L. M. Freeman, R. M. Moore, M. H. Stuart, Great Heart, Trixie, A.P. Hicks, W. B. V arn

Block 3 – Washington D.C.

Block 4 – W.K. Coleman, W.G. Langford, J. A. Herring, F. G. Colson, F. G. Bailey, A. J. Angle, R.W. Irving, J. A. Gaillard, A Keathley, '98 & '99

Block 5 – My Friend, Mrs. Shaffer, "Badahn," Will Day, Vinnie Willis, May Porter, Mrs. Crigler, Lucy Carpenter, Clare Webster, May Woodard

Block 6 – Cora Pound, H. Keigwin, HP, Toots, Myrtle Pound, Ruby Helen, Carlton Nathaniel, M.E.K.

ROW 5:

Block 1 – Little Girl.", Teeta Woodward, M. W. Brown, Mrs. L. H. Robinson, L. M. Stamps, Mr. C.H. Robinson, E. W. DeLorna, Berta Freeman, M.E. Brown, R. D. Allston

Block 2 – Mrs. S. Green, Mrs. L. Lovesey, Miss Sallie Cavanah, Mrs. A. Bushnel, Mrs. A. Lake, Mr. & Mrs. John Jackson, Mr. & Mrs. John Morton, Byron & Ashley

Block 3 – G. K. Smith, J Summerlin, Mrs. T J Lake, W.K. Bryson, H.W. Webster, Edwin Anderson, E. Oglesby, J.M. Oglesby, E.R. Wharton, Arthur Webster

Block 4 – T.G. Torry, Mrs. T.G. Torry, Daisy, Hector, James, Sallie Hate, Mrs. Jefferson Vary, Jefferson Vary, Charlotte, Mrs. Torry

Block 5 – Mr. M. Anderson, Mrs M. F. Anderson, J. M. Snedegar, Harry Anderson, Miriam Anderson, Claud McBride, Irma McBride, Mrs. A.J. Lewis, Mrs. Frank Bushnell, Mrs. F. M. Wilson

Block 6 – W. Tyler, M. E. P. Tyler, A.C. Tuttle, Dr. R. Patton, K.M. Patton, Rita, JR Langford, S.P. Harn, B. F. Harn, M. P. Harn

ROW 6:

Block 1 – 0

Block 2 – Sara E Brown, Jno. Burdine, J.N. Jackson, J.M. Lowry, L. Hebb, E.E. Montfort, E.G. Gardner, H.E. Whiteman, T.E. Cheatham, W.E. Alderman

Block 3 – J. Chas. Potter, M.P. Jordan, Mrs. C Dietrich, Mrs. I. Bivins, Mrs. A.L. Hall, Mrs. M. Bishop, J. Bishop, W H Hall, Daisy Bertles, Mrs. J.G. Scanlin

Block 4 – M. Scott, J. Harden, J. Summerlin, J M. Lanier, J. Varn, B E. Bushnell, A.T. Whaler, A. Williams, L J. Marquis, L. Willard

Block 5 – H. P. Logan, L. Willard, C.E. Edwards, A. Lowery, Lt. Johnson, W.H. Johnson, N. M. Edwards, M.E. Willard, M. Barbour

Block 6 – Mrs. China B. Smith, Adele A. Smith, A.K. Smith, E.M. Smith, Mrs. J.N. Smith, Mrs. T.B. Davis, C.W. Hoover, U.A. Minshall, J.l. Wirt, Mrs. J. S. Wirt

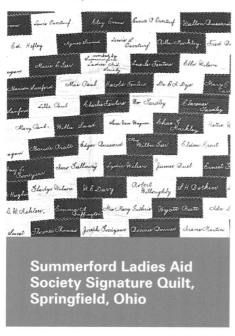

Summerford Ladies Aid Society Signature Quilt, Springfield, Ohio

ROW 1: C. E. Traphagan, Sarah J Mell., Mrs. Lizzie Buzzard, Mr. Will Goodyear, Robert Adams, Mr. A. Thayn Young, M. E. Fricker, Cora T. Tingley, Mrs. H. J. Overturf

ROW 2: Nannie Adams, Mrs. Mae Goodyear, Mrs. Alice L. Young, Mrs. M. J. Bussard, Oris Goodyear, Robert M. Hamilton, Miss Ethel M. Chance, Rolla Cartzdafner, H. T. Tingley

ROW 3: M. J. Busie, Thelma Tingley, Mrs. Henry Beathard, Seren N. Marsh, Rev. George R. Mell, Emery Goodyear, Geneva Chance, Mitchell Farmer, S.L. Turner, Mrs. Mollie Kelley

ROW 4: Mr. Frank Kelley, Fannie B. Chance, Guymeth Farmer, R.F. Traphagan, Dr. Jos. W. Chance, Maude Peterson, Walter Goodyear, Jake Benhaus, Miss Nettie Snider, George M. D. Bussard

ROW 5: Miss Ellen Ellsworth, W.E. Rice, Elsie I. Tingley, Mrs. Anna Hinton, Andrew J. Brougher, Ethel E. Rice, Ida Winfield, Mamie Ryan, Mr. Paul S. Chance, Grace Kimble

ROW 6: Helen Kimble, Mrs. Jos. W. Chance, Bernice Kimble, Gladys Hinton, E. C. Roberts, Laura Rhodes, Josie Wadkins, Mrs. John S. Holland, Mrs. M. E. Fricker, Grover Shelton

ROW 7: Nannie Roberts, E. E. Edwards, John Houston, Alice J. Farmer, Robert Paul, Mrs. Jessie Goodyear, Leonida Wragg, Elden Sweet, Madison Willoughby, C. E. Lamb

ROW 8: Hattie Edwards, Mrs. John Houston, Harry Farmer, Mrs. Robert Paul, Mr. Ulysses Goodyear, Mollie Willoughby, Marjoy Celina Young, Mrs Lizzie Kimble, Walter Traphagan, James Orebaugh

ROW 9: Mrs. Mary Keifer, Emma Brown, Stella M. Clingen, Malinda S. Clingen, Verna Castor, Lorese Goldsmith, Mae Seigfried, Laura Arnold, Ellen Bussard, Mrs. Wm. E. Teazel

ROW 10: George Goodyear, Hartford Fenters, Mrs. James Davisson, Frank Bussard, Elmer Willoughby, Mrs. Charlie Pringle, Addie Goodyear, J. Goedtian, Scott Teazel, Mary E. Mitchell

ROW 11: Walter Wilson, George Lightle, Maurice Goodyear, Philip Markley, Glenn Davisson, Blanche Mitchell, Lillian Willoughby, M. L. Burnham, Mrs. Scott Teasel, Grace Goodyear

ROW 12: Noel Mitchell, Marietta Huffey, Bessie Sweet, Wilda J. Wilson, Allen Cross, Eva Goodyear, Mrs. Nellie Buzzard, Traphagan, Prugh Overturf, Roy Sweet, Hettie Hendrix.

ROW 13: Forest Bidwell, Lester Goodyear, Jessie Fenters, Umphrey Nisewanner, Marjorie Eloise Traphagan, Mrs. Thomas Davisson, G. W. Butler, Mrs. Prugh Overturf, R. W. Boyd, Orville Willoughby

ROW 14: Mary Traphagan, Elizabeth Minshall, Grace Bussard, Dell Fanver, Sarah A. Earsom, Fred L. Newsom, Vivian T. Overturf, Ora A. Potts, Mattie Rockwell, Cecil Fenters

ROW 15: C. A. Wilson, Mrs. Jessie Deck, Mary Goodyear, Clare Evans, Lewis Overturf, Clay Evans, Everett P. Overturf, Walton Bussard, Minnie Cheseldine, Tweed Dickason

ROW 16: Mrs. Laura Makely, Clark Willoughby, Mrs. Hester Speasmaker, Ed. Hefley, Agnes Soward, Lewis S. Overturf, Rilla Markely, Fred Bostwick, Fred Bostwick, Gertrude Williams, N. C. Pitzer

ROW 17: Hattie Ackerman, Mary Bostwick, Charley Winfield David Traphagan, Marie E. Geer, worked by Summerford Ladies Aid Society, Lucile Fenters, Ella Wilson, Miss Anastasia Singleton, T. J. Prugh

ROW 18: John Wilson, Donna Evans, Frank Arbuckle, Marion Sanford, Mae Paul, Harold Fenters, Dr. E.A Dye, Mary E. Cartzdafner, Rev Hugh Smith, Mr. Clellson Markedly

ROW 19: Emma Clingen, Mrs. Esta Shack, Julia Prugh, Mrs. Marion Sanford, Lillie Paul, Charlie Fenters, Wm Yardley, Clarence Yardley, Anna Yardley, Clarence Yardley

ROW 20: George W. Cartzdafner, Jes Davisson, Mr Wilber Geer, Mary Paul, Willis Sweet, Sara Van Wagner, Chas. G. Markely, Hettie Woosley, Mrs. Ira Robbins, Katie Bostwick

ROW 21: Mrs. George Durkee, Clarance W. Potee, Ruth Buffington, Ellis Traphagan, Maude Pratt, Edgar Bussard, Mrs. William Geer, Eldon Krout, Glen W. Smith Helen Krout

ROW 22: Mr. J.G. Dhume, Mrs. Chas Markely, Charles Bales, Inez L. Goodyear, Imo Galloway, Lydia Wilson, James Buel, Ernest Green, Myrtle Arrick, Mrs. Andrew Thomas

ROW 23: Estyl Wilson, Howard Ammons, Mary Flanagan, Rev. George M. Hughes, Gladys Wilson, W. E. Davy, Robert Willoughby, S. H. Botkin, Lizzie Hamilton, Donna Ellsworth

ROW 24: Mary Rhoades, Flora Bussard, Margaret Green, L. W, Ashten, Emma A. Buffington, Mrs. Mary Guthrie, Wyatt Pratt, Ada Duhme, Rev Clink, Georgia Goodyear, Jr.

ROW 25: Mamie Ryan, Mr. W. J. Edwards, Lena McCartney, Sarah Sweet, Florence Thomas, Joseph Goodyear, Bonnie Bonner, Irene Martin, Mrs. Forest Bidwell, Ivon Barnes

ROW 26: John F. Kelley, C. E. Arbuckle, Pearl DeVore, Mrs. W. J. Edwards, Alonzo Morris, Emma Ammons, Kate Dhume Cora D, Hughes, Homer Stone, Lydia Young

ROW 27: Joseph McWhirt, Hannah Markely, John Keifer, Laura Mae Young, Auburn S. Goodyear, Alfred Kimble, Ethlyn Markely, Oris Sweet, Cora Bridgewater, Hazel Carson

ROW 28: Nettie Bussard, Horace Markely, Kate Schlesinger, Lenora B. Goodyear, Olga Spither, Walter Arrick, Hugh McCord, Estyl M. Goodyear, Albert Fisher, Francis Markely

ROW 29: IN REMEMBRANCE

ROW 30: John Hinton, Robert R. Earson, Rev. William M. Overturf, Albert Sweet, Ralph Kimble, Mr. William Bussard, Walter B. Earsom, Edward Cole, Ralph W. Hinton, Joshua Hinton

ROW 31: Rheuben Kelley, Naoma Hinton, Alice C. Sprague, Mary Soward, John H. Markely, Elizabeth Kelley, Maud Prugh, Norah Markely, Esther Markely, Eliza Nisewanner

ROW 32: Mrs. John W. Cartzdafner, Elizabeth A. Goings, John Arbuckle, Addie Clingan, Monmouth P Goodyear, Stafford Hurd, Mary E. Goodyear, Ellen Yardley, John W. Cartzdafner, Bruce Cornell

ROW 33: Thalia Virginia Nisewanner, Harley Austin Nisewanner, Clifton Halleck Nisewanner, Artie Mae Nisewanner, Sarah Elizabeth Eckels Nisewanner, Sidney Nisewanner, Anna M. Nisewanner, Nora Belle Nisewanner, Marjorie Shaffer, Eliza Jones.

ROW 34: William G. Jones, Blanche Aglaia Jones, Selsor Holden Jones, Mrs. Malinda Overturf, H. M. Comfort, Valentine Prugh, C. A. Comfort, Frances P. Fox

TOP

ROW 1: Helen Wilson, Paul C. Overturf, Gussie Hefley, Stella M. Hix, Elizabeth Ritter, Edward Geer, Stewart Ritter, Willie Overturf, Tom Golden, Thomas Morris, Emma A. Hix

ROW 2: Mary E. Arbuckle, Frank Paul, Homer Evans, Helen Clark, Bertha Overturf, J. R, Young, Mary Dhume, Mrs. Celanda Young, Mary Blue, William Hix, Mr. J. W. DeVore, Bessie Young, Homer Trueax

ROW 3: Louise Morris, Mrs. Grace Lanheater, Hazel Pratt, Alonzo Thomas, Eunice Geer, William Soward, Anna Grant, Margaret B. Chance, William Holland, Chella Buffington, Ella M. Coons, Noah Hutslar, Fay Morris

BOTTOM

ROW 1: Mary Cornell, Emma Arvilla Nisewanner Jones, David Selson Jones, Sidney Selson Shaffer, Spencer reed Shaffer, John Milton Shaffer, Stella west Barber, Millard Gist, Brantford Gist, Eloise Cornell, Effie McCorkle

ROW 2: Frank Kiefer, Mrs. Rebecca Wilson, Mr. C. J. Lankester, Delpine Holland, Alice Golden, Effie Evans, Joseph Hock, Robert Overturf, Donald Keith Cornell, Jennie M. Cornell, Emma Holland, Margaret Bennett

ROW 3: Charley Tingley, Myrtle Tingley, Oscar Tingley, Robert A. Bussard, Ellen Bunton, Ideal Art Co. Springfield, Ohio, Charlie Kelley, Marcus Cornell, Sarah Grant, Charles Yardley, Thomas

SIDE 1

ROW 1: Ella Bunton, A. B. Orebaugh, Eva Wilson, Robert C. Harbage, Bertha Fields, Charlie Nicewarner, Edward Betts, Robert Lewis Coberly, D.C. Blue, Rilla Markely, Miss Virginia R. Culpepper, Maurice L. Sweet, Nellie E. Sweet, Rilla Hornbeck, Clara Bridgewater, Mrs. J. N. Marsh

ROW 2: Francis Guthrie, Chester Prugh, North Pitzer Marra J. Fauver, Elwood Prugh, Rebecca Wilson, Minnie Hock, Andrew Hock, Ada B. Chance, Mrs. Clyde Gist, Flora Thomas, Edna Grant, George Wm. Prugh, Jessie E, Chance, Nettie Fisher, Ruth Tingley, Geraldine Tingley

SIDE 2

ROW 1: Laura Geer, Clara M. Sweet, H. H. Johnson, Elizabeth A. Kelley, Fannie Alder, Wilbert Hinton, Charles Kimble, Clara Edwards, Jeanette Guthrie, Clark e. Hix, Dr. M. C. Sprague, Maud Haffey, Paul Markley, Ira Robbins, Warren Markley, James Guthrie

ROW 2: Robert Theodore Wilson, Herbert Bendel, Charley Prugh, Joseph Pratt, Josephine Prugh, Ruth Bendel, Gus Prugh, Bruce M. Sweet, Myrtle Pitzer, Herbert Guthrie, Glenna Kimble, Josie Wilson, Asa Hinton, Lamar P. Wilson, Dr. J. W. Dixon, Fred Guthrie, Roselle Dhume

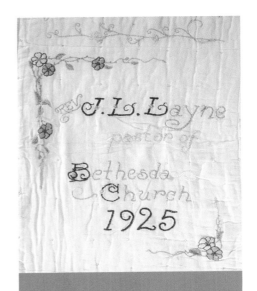

Signature Presentation Quilt, United Methodist Church, Rev. J.L. Layne pastor of Bethesda Church, 1925, Ono, West Virginia

ROW 1:

Block 1 – Center – Freely ye have received, Freely give. Ava MacIntire, Homer Glenn, Lou Holly, John Wolford, Lee Turner, J C Hicks, Ellen Ash, Mitt Meyers, Mattie Smith, Lou Holly, Tom Clark, I. J. Ashworth, J. W. Chapman, Y. W. Stepheson, Marie Black, Iva Black, James Jordan, Ada Jordan

Block 2 – Mr. and Mrs. Met. Gore, W. E. Vaughan, Edgar Cozad, Orin Slagle, Henry Taylor, J. T. Roberts, George Morris, Clyde Chapman, Ruth Tomlinson, P R Jones, M St. Adkins, Frances Cozad, Mae Taylor, Oakley Dick, Mamie Roberts, Maude Morris, M. Damron, M. Clark, E. Bowyer

Block 3 – W. H. Yates, S. L. Handley, Emma Morrison, B E Morrison, Lee Bell, J L McDonnie, B K McDonnie, W C Hager, F R Roberts, M J Handley, Frank Morrison, Carrie Morrison, L D Martin, A B Martin, S E McDonnie, Clara Jordan, Emma Martin, Ollie Hager, C A Jordan, Phil Murray, Felix Yo???

Block 4 – Sylvia Reynolds, Thurman Mounts, H L Mounts, ???Juanita Mounts, Clara Birch, Jemel Hatton, Edmond Glenn, V S Stewart, M A Stewart, S E Mounts, F W Mounts, E L Mounts, Kate Collins, Violet Milkiff, G S Dolin, A B Glenn, Lydia Glenn, Sam Markin, G F Rader

ROW 2:

Block 1 – Eulah Stallman, D. N. Bell, Mable Jackson, Inez Litton, W R L???, John Blackwood, Sam Heller, Ida Hollister, H. C. Heck, Charley Wilkinson, Roy Baumgardner, Clyde Harshlarger, Lizzie Yates, M. A. Mart???, Cecil Dillon, Clettie Maddox, Dea. Blackwood, Molly L????, Maud Glenn, Anna Harshlarger, Osna Marta???, Halley Wilkinson, Louisa Harshlarger

Block 2 – Evan Newman, F J Wood, Cora Newman, C R Taylor, Mary Taylor, Claude Dick, Lola Dick, J M Shaffer, Alice Scarberry, L Webb, Arnold Cyrus, Bertram Hughes, Sydney Hughes, G. Roberts, Lydia Roberts, E. Rallyson, Bevard Lemley, Lottie Lemley, Robert Ashwood, A. Beavers

Block 3 – Rudolph Cooper, Hanagard Cooper, Mr. and Mrs. R. M. Morris, Elmer Arnold, Ottmer Morris, Berman Cooper, Earl Weeks, Mr. and Mrs. P. Weeks, Mr. and Mrs. L. Wells, Mr. and Mrs. C. M. Love, Mr. and Mrs. G. B. Comer, Thelma Comer, Asa Cooper, Fred Kincaid, Alta Kincaid, Mr. and Mrs. C L McClary, Jim Kincaid, Hutson Cooper

Block 4 – Lee Turner, June Alkins, Elva Alkins, M A Bell, Lester Stevens, Gladys Bell, Ecil??? Suttle, Frank Cox, Mrs. J. Layne, Susan Stowasser, Roy Rimmer, Ernest Harles, Agnes M Stowasser, M J Reynolds, W A Reynolds, Mr. and Mrs. Sampson

ROW 3:

Block 1 – F. W. Gwinn, G W Eskew, C. R. Hatfield, Matilda Hatfield, Jesse Collins, James Suttler, Mr and Mrs Harry Kent, Johnnie Ball, Alice Ball, Mr and Mrs M F Fuller, Mr and Mrs J A Everett, Mr and Mrs Urie Holley, Mr and Mrs G Reynolds, Mr and Mrs J Reynolds, R Yeater

Block 2 – Harry M. Herndon, Mr and Mrs M. F. Adkins, Mr and Mrs J. A. Glenn, Rosie Glenn, Mary Glenn, Effie Glenn, Mr and Mrs Clarence Sowards, Mr and Mrs E. C. Handley, Reverend William Bias

Block 3 – Rev. J. L. Layne pastor of Bethesda Church 1925

Block 4 – B. E. Morrison, Caria Morrison, Carl Mohr, Loyd Lucas, M Morrsion, Lucion Bell, Virgil Ball, A M Reynolds, F M Kurly, J M Roberts, C E Adkins, M B Adkins, Virginia Blackwood, J F gross, Kath Gross, Tom Perry, Mildred Shamlin

ROW 4:

Block 1 – W. A. Martin, J. G. Thacker, Mrs. J. G. Thacker, C. W. McDorrie, M. E. McDorrie, Mr. and Mrs. S. R. McDorrie, L. R. McDorrie, Woodrow McDorrie, W. C. McDorrie, M. F. McDorrie, Mr. and Mrs. L. R. Via, Junior Via, C. J. McDorrie

Block 2 – Shelby J Love age 87, Mrs. Shelby J. Love, Anna Love, Mr and Mrs E Love, Marion Love, Frances Love, Edward Love, Mr and Mrs Pew, Shelba Glenn Pew, Mary Stinerman, Mr and Mrs O Stinerman, Helene Stinerman, Margie Stinerman, Starry Stinerman

Block 3 – B Napier, Rosey Napier, Ivan Tomlinson, G. Blake, A.J. Marrs, Brady Hughes, Emzy Stickler, H Adkins, E Crouch, Pauline Crouch, H. D. Largey, C. H. Newman, Mr. and Mrs. R A Asher, B. F. Childers, J. W. Tomlinson, Mr and Mrs B. L. Hager

Block 4 – Mr. and Mrs. E. Ward, Mr and Mrs C. E. Myers, Edna Myers, Tom Myers, Cecil Davis, Jack Ward, Leona Ward, F Dalton, Helen Ann Ward, age 4 Martha, Frances Ward, Emogene Ward, Lena Cyrus, Locie Cyrus, Wyatt Dillon, C. E. Smith, Edna Smith, Irwin Loyeans, L. H. Perkins, Harry Gorby, L. Woodward

ROW 5:

Block 1 – Wm Bard, Ethel Bard, Julian Bell, Eva Mullins, Herbert Smith, Millard Bird, Roy Roberts, Pansy Bird, Sesco Sovard, T P Sovard. Elsie Reynolds, Louisa Sowards, H P Bird, Walter Bias, Ray Bird, Merry Xmas

Block 2 – Mr and Mrs. Frank Adkins, Mr. and Mrs C. T. Bowyer, Clyde Crouch, W. Coffman, Mrs. Cecil Traylor, L. Coffman, Mrs. Harry Hobinson, Mr and Mrs Willie Soward, Mr and Mrs Hugh Forth, Mr and Mrs S. Cooper, Edwin Cooper, E.A. Taylor, J G Carper, Mrs O. Slagle, Mr and Mrs Wm Kirby

Block 3 – H. G. Templeton, Ben Blake, Mr. and Mrs. F Cooper, S. G. Wilson, E A Wilson, Laura Beaver, E. C. Halley, Mr and Mrs J. W. Eagan, Mr and Mrs H F Wood, Mr and Mrs S. E. Baumgardner, James T. Cozad, Hazel Lewis, Morris Blake, B. F. Lemley, L. E. Synder, Bailey Halley

1939 Progressive Gleaners Quilt Top, North Campbell and Springfield, Missouri

ROW 1: Marie K., Frances Johns, Marie White, Mrs. M. E. Wallis, June Johns, Ada Sherpy

ROW 2: Mrs. Ketchum, Ida Campbell, Marida White, Auntie Welch, Nellie Hamilton, Victoria

ROW 3: Alice Wommack, Bessie Martin, Olive Martin, Progressive Gleaners 1939, Auntie Johns, Velma Hamilton

ROW 4: Pauline Payne, Ruth White, Bessie Ward, Mrs. Nell Wolkins, Mrs. B. L. Goodwin, Alice Sherpy

ROW 5: Betty Lou, Pearl Wommack, Theresa Farmer, Mrs. Payne, Mrs. Alice Conn, Alta

Windsor Evangelical Church Ladies Bible Class Quilt, Windsor, York, Pennsylvania

COLUMN 1: J. K. Wineholt, Russel Witmer, Jr., Glen Witmer, Robert Witmer, Donald Witmer, Spurgeon Knisley, William

Knisley, Neva Fake, Charlotte Fake, Ella Winters, Clare Miller, Countess Miller, Robert Miller, Annie Herman, Ida Butcher, Virgie Horn, Blanche Herman, Grace Smith, Susan Collins, Beulah Stein, Bertha Sechrist, Marie Sechrist, Samuel Ness, Mary Ness, Clarence Gibson, Horace Gibson, Madalyn Gibson, Gloria Oberdorff, Mary Oberdorff, Terry Godrey, Paul Heindel, Roy Reider, Reverend and Mrs. H. A. Snook, Simon Oberdorff, Samuel Knaub, Helen Knaub, LaMar Knaub, William Fake, John Hoffmaster, Jessie Bahn, Harvey Kilgore, Maggie Kilgore, Carl Kilgore, Laura Sargen, Maggie Flinchbaugh, Elizabeth Brennaman, Affes Resh, Orrie Baker, William Attlesberg, Grace Baily, Jacob Frey, Arabella Floyd, Anna Keller, Grace Grim

COLUMN 2: Kenneth Ness, William Flinchbaugh, Carrie Flinchbaugh, Margaret Mellinger, Arthur Heindel, Maggie Heindel, Sarah Heindel, Harvey Smith, Nettie Smith, Flossie Buckingham, Harry Paules, Bertha Paules, Ilene Paules, Kurvin Smith, Alverta Smith, Virginia Schnetzka, Clarence Flinchbaugh, Mattie Flinchbaugh, Katherine Flinchbaugh, Sarah Ellis, Quinton Ellis, Blanch Stein, Earl Heindel , Irma Oberdorff, Ruth Flinchbaugh, Frederick Flinchbaugh, Glen Flinchbaugh, Estella Oldhouser, Mamie Holtzinger, Esther DeShong, Helen DeShong, Miriam Reichard, Thelma Schnetzka, Paul Collins, Emma Collins, Romane Reichard, Phillip Reichard, Catura Smeltzer, Ruth Krewson, Lizzie Dieffendaffer, Ida Kauffman, Mildred Theophel, Earnestine Bahn, Leola Reider, Martha Kise, Maggie Poff, Velma Smith, Alverta Snyder, Helen Gipe, Horace Gipe, Jewel Gipe, Margie Lease, Elma Reider, Rosie Smith

COLUMN 3:
Top – Dema Reichard, Bertha Ness, Mabel Howard, Charles Olphin, Milton Spyker, Carrie Ebert, Herman Ebert, Ella Crawford
Bottom – Gertie Silar, Delores Silar, Samuel Silar, Dean Reider, Mary Graham, Gloria Graham, Curtis Silar, Carrie Silar, Martha Olewiler, Preston Stump

COLUMN 4:
Top – Wayne Godfrey, Curvin Paules, Mary Paules, William Graybill, Mary Graybill, Mary Boeckel, Oscar Paules, Malilda Paules, Bertha Collins, Frederick Collins
Bottom – Margaret Ehrhart, Betty Bell, John Slenker, Carrie Hoffmaster, Arvilla Oberdorff, Nora Oberdorff, Annie Oberdorff, Elmer Oberdorff, Mabel Oberdorff, Faye Paul

COLUMN 5:
Top – Palmer Smith, Myrtle Smith, Eugene Smith, Viola Ruby, Betty Ruby, Carolyn Ruby, Austin Smeltzer, Ruth Smeltzer, Delores Collins, Charles Ferres
Bottom – Charles Oberdorff, Preston Oberdorff, Margaret Oberdorff, Blanche Resline, Ruth Resline, Joyce Resline, Nellie Stein, Kenneth Zorbaugh, Wayne Sweger, Catherine Stegner

COLUMN 6:
Top – Helen Poff, Dean Poff, Carl Poff, Rietta Wallace, Agnes Spyker, Maggie Knaub, Olene Smith, Mae Myers
Bottom – Iris Gentzler, Barbara Knisely, Capitola Bull, Betty Hartman, Sarah Gohn, Helen Clouser, Verna Olphin, Lillian Hershner, Estella Bell, Ida Welsh

COLUMN 7:
Bottom – Elwood Paul Jr., Mae Paul, Ognetta Bell, Jimmie Reider, Norma Reider, Joan Reider, Arsula Snyder, Alverta Reider, Nettie Smith, Doris Keller

COLUMN 8:
Bottom – Glenn Sterner, Francis Sterner, Jolene Sterner, Charles Omer, Park Holtzinger, Robert Holtzinger, Flossie Holtzinger, Glenda Swords, C.P. Smeltzer, Barbara Kook

COLUMN 9: Anna Young, Belva Wilhelm, Josiah Meads, Jerome Flinchbaugh, Ella Flinchbaugh, James Flinchbaugh, Lucille Gentzler, Mae Miller, Mildred Miller, Naomi Myers, Viola Olewiler, Claude Hivner, Orfa Hiver, Doris Hivner, Patricia Hivner, Ella Blouse, E.H. Forry, C.E. Flinchbaugh, David Emenheiser, Annie Emenheiser, Mervin Ellis, Ida E. Knaub, Flora Flinchbaugh, Dale Resline, Junior Resline, Harry Smeltzer, Flora Smeltzer, Harry Wolf, Emma Wolf, Minnie Montgomery, Henry Wolf, Henry Holtzinger, Annie Holtzinger, Wilson Heindel, Kenneth K. Poet, Mary Poet, Kenneth E. Poet, Mardella Flinchbaugh, Ida Sietz, Lester Kinard, Francelia Kinard, Barry Kinard, Spurgeon Coyeman, Verna Coyeman, Charles Coyeman, Jennie Koontz, Curvin Markel, Corena Markel, Clair Markel, George Shaw, Evan Shaw, Louise Shaw, Norma Sh

COLUMN 10: Isabelle Baker, Rae Baker, Ella Baker, Lester Sprenkle, Amanda Sprenkle, Helen Ness, F.M. Meads, Maggie Meads, Jacqueline Deitz, Faye Mellinger, J.Kenneth Laucks, J. Kenneth Laucks, Jr., Vera Laucks, Walter Stein, Linnie Stein, Kenneth Stein, Harry Creek, Sanie Creek, Gladys Creek, Blanch Arnold, Mary Oberdorff, Flora Herman, Helen Herman, James Herman, Orfa Wise, Rosella Grim, Elmer Herman,

W. M. Koontz, Cora E. Flinchbaugh, R. F. Flinchbaugh, Romane Emenheiser, Janet Holtzinger, Perry Hoffmaster, Emma Hoffmaster, Kaye Francis Hoffmaster, Hilda Burk, Elizabeth Butcher, Minnie Warner, Mabel Flinchbaugh, Eva Kilgore, Jimmie Koontz, Clara Brammer, Darilene Shoff, Doris Shoff, Bud Shoff, Malinda Shoff, Vera Shoff, Mary Conrad, Charles Conrad, Edith Funk, Henrietta Minnich, Grace Gibbs, Charles Gibbs, Rufus Kann, Mary Elizabeth Fellenbaum.

Oklahoma Bible Signature Quilt, c. 1950

Machine pieced, hand embroidered, hand quilted, 69 inches X 84 inches, cotton
ROW 1: Zelma Nickel, Ps.86:15; Marion Goertzer, Psalm 27:1; Louise Wiebe, Isaiah 55:9,11; Adeline Penner Psalm 100
ROW 2: Eileen Lowen, Psalms 21:1; Mrs. Bill G. Wiebe, Is. 12-2; Mrs. Paul Redekop, Psalm 37-5; Verna Buhler, Isa 40:31
ROW 3: Susie Unger, John 3; Mrs. Nick J. Dyck, John 15:7; Elizabeth Enns, Psalms 36-7; Lydia Peters, Ps. 91
ROW 4: Adina Martens, Matt 18:19; Mrs. Wm Niessen, Isaiah 40:31; Mrs. F. Hopper, 1 Cor. 15:58; Irma Unger, Heb. 4:16
ROW 5: Mrs. Dave Sawatzky Jer.33:3, Mrs. Clarence Williams, Job 23:10

Index

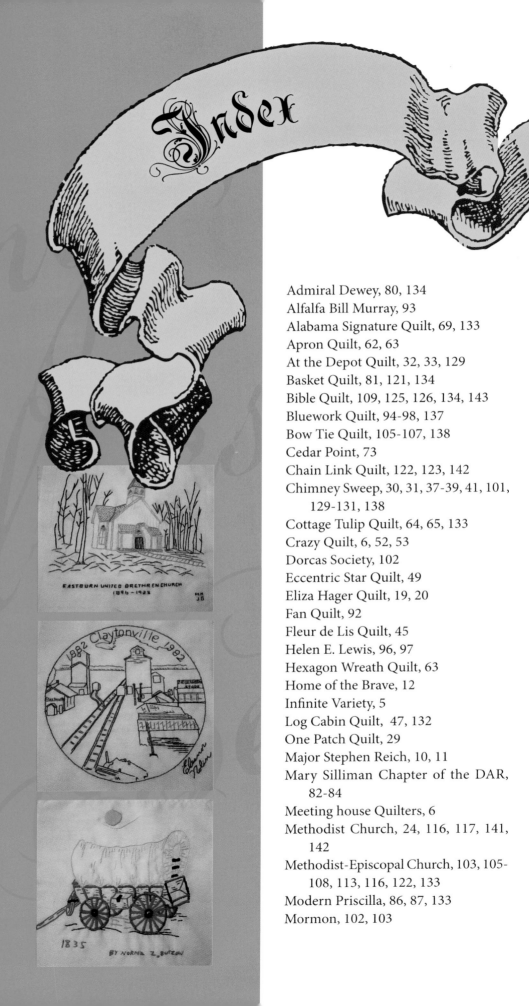